TREE SPIKER

SPIKER

From **Earth First!** to **Lowbagging:**

My Struggles in Radical
Environmental Action

MIKE ROSELLE

with Josh Mahan

ST. MARTIN'S PRESS ❧ NEW YORK

www.stmartins.com

Book design by Phil Mazzone

Library of Congress Cataloging-in-Publication Data

Roselle, Mike.
  Tree spiker : from Earth First! to lowbagging: my struggles in radical environmental action / Mike Roselle with Josh Mahan.
      p. cm.
   ISBN 978-0-312-55619-8
  1. Deep ecology.   2. Environmentalism.   3. Environmental protection.
4. Conservation of natural resources.   5. Earth First! (Organization)
I. Mahan, Josh.   II. Title.
   GE195.R67   2009
   333.72—dc22

                                                          2009016937

First Edition: October 2009

10 9 8 7 6 5 4 3 2 1

For Delores Ann

CONTENTS

ACKNOWLEDGMENTS

The decision to write a book should never be taken too seriously. Josh Mahan and I made the decision while running the whitewater rapids on the Main Salmon River in Idaho's River of No Return Wilderness. The words here are mostly mine, but I never could have produced a book without Josh's help. Using his incredible skills to intimidate and shame me, he kept me working when I would otherwise be slacking off. He also pushed for the precision and accuracy in this text that his trade as a journalist demands.

No book could do justice to the brave women and men in whose company I have had the honor of serving. This book is not an attempt to fully document the movement with which I am so proud to be involved. Many important events and people go unmentioned for no particular reason other than lack of space and a faulty memory. Think of this work as more of a series of campfire tales and late-night bar talk. Someday the full story will be told, and it will undoubtedly be even weirder than the one you are about to read here.

I would especially like to thank Adam Chromy of Artists and Artisans. Without his advice and encouragement, this book would have never been written. Also, my gratitude goes out to Phil Knight, Howie Wolke, and Jake Kreilick, who previewed sections of the manuscript. Thanks to J. R., Twilly, and Gruver for just being there, and to Wayne Fairchild and the entire Lewis and Clark Trail Adventures family, who made sure I got away from the computer and out into the wilderness once in a while. Also to Pam Wellner, Tracy Katelman, and Atosa Soltani, who provided valuable research and camaraderie for over two decades as part of the Rainforest Action Network's forest action team. And to Karen Pickett, Claire Greensfelder, Kristin Nelson, Meglana Lubenova, Sarah Perry, and Laura Caskey for putting up with me through thick and thin.

In addition, I would like to thank Allen Gunn for providing crucial technical support to Josh and me to get the Web site Lowbagger.org off the ground. The writings on that site eventually led to this book.

I'd also like to thank Jim Flynn, Lauren Reagan, Steve Marsden, Andy Kerr, Celia Landman, Celia Alerio, Joe Hickey, Jasper Carleton, and Peter Bahouth for their tireless efforts in standing up to the government agencies and corporations who illegally plunder this planet for short-term gain.

FOREWORD

Radicalism in American Environmental History

By Dr. Roderick Nash

Roderick Frazier Nash is Professor Emeritus of History and Environmental Studies at the University of California–Santa Barbara. He is recognized as a creator of the field of environmental history and the author of Wilderness and the American Mind *(2001) and* The Rights of Nature: A History of Environmental Ethics *(1989).*

Writing in 1787, as his new nation took shape, Benjamin Rush observed that "the American war is over: but this is far from being the case with the American revolution. On the contrary, nothing but the first act of the great drama is closed." The second act might be thought of as the abolition of slavery; subsequent ones addressed the rights of women, native people, and the gay community. Freedom was as American as apple pie, and oppressed minorities did relatively well under the democratic New World sun. This book describes the beginnings of the most recent wave of reform, which advocated extending ethical standing to the nonhuman world, including endangered species and even rivers and forests. In the minds of these reformers, the natural rights idea needed to be expanded once again: this time the objective was the rights of nature.

The environmental movement that a young Mike Roselle entered in the early 1970s took place in an exciting historical context. The pent-up materialism lingering in the United States from the 1930s Depression and World War II had faded. To the beat of a different kind of music known as "rock and roll," a new generation started to question basic American axioms. A major one concerned the status of nature in our civilization. Spearheaded by Rachel Carson (*Silent Spring,* 1962), Paul Ehrlich (*The Population Bomb,* 1968), and the rediscovery of Aldo Leopold's *A Sand County Almanac* (1949), awareness spread that growth was not synonymous with progress and that an expanding technological civilization was, in fact, tearing apart the fabric of the ecosystem. A remarkable series of laws gave the nation a system of dedicated wilderness areas (1964), banned dams in the Grand Canyon (1968), and protected endangered species (1973). Meanwhile, astronauts circled the moon and brought back images of a tiny, vulnerable "spaceship earth."

The people featured in Mike's account were driven by a sense of moral outrage at their species' relationship to the natural world. Sure, Theodore Roosevelt was angry about the frontier-inspired wastefulness of wildlife and forests, and his 1908 proposal of "conservation" launched a political crusade. And John Muir believed the 1913 approval of a dam in Yosemite National Park's spectacular Hetch Hetchy Valley was an affront to both nature and God. But these protests were very anthropocentric and stopped with efforts to reform the destructive system. Environmental ethics raised the stakes and made reformers radicals and even revolutionaries. There was a taste of what was to come in Henry David Thoreau's 1849 declaration that "if . . . the machine of government . . . is of such a nature that it requires you to be the agent of injustice to another, then, I say, break the law." Thoreau was, in writing this, concerned about a form of domination and exploitation called slavery, but he also believed the American treatment of wild nature was ethically wrong. Observing the effect of a New England dam on spawning shad, he declared himself on the side of the migratory fish and wondered if a crowbar was the proper tool for solving the problem. No doubt Thoreau would have been an enthusiastic reader of Edward Abbey's *The Monkey Wrench Gang* (1975) and joined Earth First! in its 1981 action against Glen Canyon Dam on the Colorado River.

The idea of wilderness is central in understanding the new priorities of Mike Roselle and the Lowbaggers. For much of American history, there was too much wilderness for appreciation to flourish. Wildness was an enemy. The pioneer purpose was to break the will of "self-willed" (or wild) environments and peoples. Axes, rifles, and barbed wire—and more recently, railroads, dams, and freeways—were the celebrated tools of an environmental transformation that left the wilderness in scattered remnants. But this very fact, symbolized by the ending of the frontier in 1890, carried with it the seeds of changing attitude. Maybe what really needed to be conquered was not the wilderness but rather our technological, capitalistic culture in its cancerlike tendency to self-destruct. Initially, the rationale for wilderness protection was almost entirely anthropocentric. Scenery, recreation, and the economics of a new nature-based tourism underlay the growing popularity of national parks and wilderness areas. Anthropocentrism and instrumentalism ruled. What set Mike apart from this was his understanding that wild places and wild things had intrinsic value, that their protection was not about *us* at all. Rather, wilderness was a place where our species took a badly needed "time out" from our ten-thousand-year-old obsession with control and modification of the planet. In honoring wilderness, we demonstrated a rare capacity for restraint. Preserved wilderness was a gesure of planetary modesty, a way to share the spaceship. It's important to keep this perspective in mind in reading about the causes and actions Mike Roselle describes. He did not go into the Nevada desert, the Oregon forests, or the hills of Appalachia to protect opportunities for outdoor recreation. I believe that in putting earth first, Mike sees himself as defending these places for their own sake.

A historical perspective is frequently kind to the reputation of radicals. Times and values change, and yesterday's threats become tomorrow's heroes. The men who dumped a million dollars' worth of tea into the Boston Harbor on the night of December 16, 1773, were reviled at the time as hooligans. But after independence, the thugs became American patriots with postage stamps and beer (Sam Adams) named in their honor. Similarly abolitionists were initially vilified, even in the North, as enemies of property and social order. It may be that environmental ethics and ecocentrism will one day rewrite the laws again. Keep that in mind as you read in the pages that follow about the birth pangs of a new morality.

Science and philosophy are increasingly aware that we stand today at the crossroads not merely of human history but of the entire evolutionary process, as well. Life evolved on this planet from stardust, water, and fire over billions of years until one clever species developed the capacity to bring down the whole biological miracle. But amidst the fear associated with this reality of a sinking ark, there is one comfort: Earth is not threatened as in the age of the dinosaurs by an errant asteroid, a death star. Now *we* are the death star, and we have an opportunity to change its course.

Imagine this planet, in the desperate frame of mind recent history warrants, sending a personals advertisement out into intestellar space: TEMPERATE BUT ENDANGERED PLANET. ENJOYS WEATHER, PHOTOSYNTHESIS, EVOLUTION, CONTINENTAL DRIFT. SEEKS CARING RELATIONSHIP WITH INTELLIGENT LIFE-FORM. Perhaps it could still be us. Perhaps we could turn from being a cancerous to a caring presense. As evidence, we might submit Mike Roselle's book.

TREE SPIKER

1

Mighty Oak

The sun was going down over the United States military's number one top-secret base. From where I stood, I could see into the town of Mercury, a town so hush-hush that buses carrying in workers from Las Vegas didn't even have windows. North of Mercury was a view of Frenchman's Flats, where the military tested its arsenal of nuclear bombs. Ronald Reagan was president, and the Cold War was at its height.

Welcome to the Nevada Test Site. It was the evening of April 7, 1986. In eighteen days, the Chernobyl Nuclear Power Plant will have a major reactor meltdown, spewing vast amounts of radioactivity across the U.S.S.R. and world. That evening, though, politics were still entrenched firmly in a pre-Chernobyl nuclear reality. So I was trying to hike into ground zero as part of a Greenpeace team to stop the Mighty Oak nuclear test from happening.

In the early stage of nuclear testing, bombs were detonated

in the atmosphere. By 1986, they were detonating the nukes at the bottoms of wells drilled deep into the desert floor. The result was more than six hundred craters pocking the desert floor, some a half mile wide, from the nuclear explosions that had been set off by the Department of Energy.

The sun continued to drop over this wasteland, and I readied to get back to work. I was high above the testing grounds, on a steep cliff, more than fifty miles from where we had been dropped off. It had been a long walk. We had hiked around Groom Lake, an area once known as Area 51, and then into a narrow canyon leading into the Jumbled Hills. It really hadn't been that hard to infiltrate the renowned military base—just a few strands of barbed wire.

Ever since it was first created as the place to blow off nukes, the Nevada Test Site has been the focus of intense opposition. To begin with, the ranchers who used to live in the region didn't want to sell their land to the government. After the aboveground tests began, the people downwind started complaining of health problems and said their animals were dying from radiation exposure. Protests began immediately and eventually pushed the tests underground by forcing the United States and Russia to sign a treaty banning atmospheric tests.

Back here in the Jumbled Hills, overlooking the test site, we heard the *thunk-thunk-thunk* of a chopper on patrol. About ten miles away and a thousand feet below us, a chopper slowly worked its way up the sandy canyon we had just hiked. In the low light of dusk, the half-inch indentations of our footprints were casting visible shadows. The jig was up.

As the helicopter proceded up the draw, we looked for a place to hide. The vegetation was scant. There were no rocks, and no features of any kind to hide in or under. It was just a high, dry ridgeline. I sat next to a flimsy creosote bush, feeling a little exposed, and waited. It was nearly dark.

More helicopters flew over us to the summit of the ridge and circled back. I was spotted, and a helicopter trained a high-powered floodlight on me. I felt like a frog in the swamp. I stood up to face the blast of air coming off the rotors.

Suddenly behind me, I heard a soldier yell, "Don't move or I'll shoot! Put your hands above your head."

I turned around to face him. He had jumped out of the helicopter before it circled around. Other soldiers had unloaded along the ridgetop, and I could see the rest of my team being rounded up.

With his gun trained on me, the soldier was backlit in the glowing light of the fading sunset. At that very moment, the ammo clip fell out of his M-16 and onto the ground. He gave me a quizzical look and shrugged his shoulders.

"You know who we are?" I asked.

"Yeah, you're Greenpeace," he replied frankly. "We've been out here looking for you for three days. We were about to go home."

Then he asked to borrow my flashlight. I obliged.

By now it was dark, and he signaled his location to the other soldiers. Eventually we were all loaded into the back of four-wheel-drive pickups, blindfolded with our hands bound, and driven down into Mercury.

Once in town, we were placed in the command center of the cat-and-mouse game we had been playing since announcing our plans to hike to ground zero and interfere with the bomb test. The command post was in a large room with a table, coffeepot, chairs, and some radio equipment. The soldiers were tired, but friendly enough.

"Are there any more of you?" one of them asked.

"No," I answered truthfully. "You got all of us. We were pretty much out of food and water anyway."

Eric, our campaign director, asked, "If we're under arrest, we need to call our attorney and ask him to be present before we answer any more questions."

"Go ahead," the soldier said. "You can use the phone on the desk."

Eric picked up the receiver and made the call. Back in our hotel room in Las Vegas, the phone rang.

Peter, our press officer, picked up. Instead of talking to our lawyer, Eric gives the green light for Plan B. The B Team is deployed as we sit in the command center.

Plan A had been a stealth attempt to get in under radar. Plan B was going to be a full-throttle race into ground zero, driving in on a network of ranch roads above the test site.

At first, the B Team tried driving in without headlights, but the endeavor proved too slow and difficult. The lights came on, and they sped down the gravel road, quickly becoming lost in the crisscrossed network of unmarked and unmapped roads. Again pink filled the skies. The sun was starting to come up, and the bomb test was set for 8 A.M. Tension began to rise. If the team couldn't make it into the test site, there would be more devastation—the nuclear blast would occur.

Just then an air force security vehicle neared the caravan of antinuclear activists.

An officer approached. "What are you doing out here, and where are you going?" he asked mechanically.

"We're a tour group looking for wild horses," Jim Puckett, the lead Greenpeace driver, coolly retorted.

"Oh, you want to go that way," the officer said, pointing

north. "Just make sure you don't go down this road. It leads right into the bombing range." With that, the security officer got in his truck and drove off.

The caravan raced along as the sun came up, now sure of their direction. Soon they saw the test site boundary—and a squadron of hovering helicopters at the gate blocking their path. The caravan slammed on its brakes. Activists piled out, trying to put on their packs and run. Once again, the helicopters had offloaded soldiers behind the vehicle, and these soldiers now surrounded the caravan.

"Don't move or we'll shoot!" the soldiers yelled once again.

Steve Loper looked the closest soldier straight in the eye. The stare down lasted only a moment before Loper said to the gunman, "You won't shoot me. I'm from Greenpeace." With that, he took off running down a nearby steep slope covered in piñon pine and juniper trees. He was gone in an instant. Three or four soldiers immediately plunged after him, crashing through the dense thorny forest.

B Team had managed to make it within spitting distance of ground zero, and a massive search was now under way for Loper. By the time Steve was discovered clinging to a tree, the countdown had to be canceled. It was the first time antinuclear activists had ever been able to delay a nuclear-weapons test anywhere in the world.

Eventually I was taken to the county jail with the A and B Teams, charged with criminal trespass, and released to the glare of television cameras broadcasting the story worldwide.

Two days later, April 10, the Mighty Oak test was conducted in the tunnels of Rainier Mesa. The nuke was detonated in a huge pipe drilled into the side of the mesa. Part of the test was to determine how well space and military hardware could withstand a nuclear blast. The doors and seals failed, releasing significant levels of radioactive Xenon 133, detected fifty miles away. The blast also vaporized most of the monitoring system and contaminated a large section of the tunnel network, setting the Star Wars program back years.

The Department of Energy was playing with fire. That's why we had tried to stop them.

Soon, Congress would pass a bill making such detonations illegal. Reagan would sign it.

The Department of Energy would deny anything had gone wrong with the Mighty Oak blast for three weeks, and even censured the Russians when Chernobyl released massive amounts of radiation into the atmosphere. When the DOE did fess up, the announcement was overshadowed by the world's reaction to Chernobyl, even though Mighty Oak rained more radiation on American soil than Chernobyl did.

This was just another day at the office with Greenpeace.

The purpose of actions such as the hike into ground zero was to confront some of the most serious environmental challenges of our time through the use of nonviolent direct action. We then provided dramatic images of these actions to the news media to grab the attention of people sitting on their couches, gobbling up otherwise approved programming.

Since 9/11, environmental groups have been wary of such confrontations, choosing instead to appear more reasonable. But with the advent of global warming and the need to address the out-of-control burning of coal and other fossil fuels, this tactic is a mistake. It will certainly take actions like those of Greenpeace to motivate the public to apply more pressure on the government to seek real climate-change solutions.

2

Hippies, Yippies, and Zippies

I never wanted to be an activist. I wanted to work as an artist, as a crewman on a tugboat, or maybe as a garbage man. But never an activist. Protesters were on television all the time. They were usually college kids getting beat up by the cops. But all that changed in 1968, when my family moved from Louisville, Kentucky, to Los Angeles, California.

Actually it was the second time we moved to L.A. We first moved out there in 1966 and returned to Louisville when my mother decided she didn't like California. After one year back in Louisville, she decided she didn't much care for Kentucky, either. So we drove back to L.A. with my four brothers and two sisters in a '59 Mercury station wagon pulling a U-Haul filled with everything we owned. In 1968, Louisville was in a steep economic decline and embroiled in a struggle between its African-American and white citizens, which occasionally brought the National Guard to our fair city to keep the peace.

I was enrolled as a student in Edgewood Junior High School in La Puente, California, when a friend of mine by the name of Michael Stevenson suggested that if I was opposed to the Vietnam War, I should wear a black armband on May Day. I did, but not so much from my opposition to the war. I had been all for the war ever since watching John Wayne in *The Green Berets* at the drive-in. I wore the armband because I didn't have very many friends and I wanted to be accepted into some group. This had been the first offer of inclusion. It would turn out to be a very small group—three of us total. But they forced me to take a position against the war, something I had not done yet.

Most of what I knew about the war was from the newspapers and television. Peace was around the corner, the news said, and America could not afford to lose a war, no matter what the reason for starting it was. This was a war against Communism, and to be against the war was to be for Communism. I didn't really know what Communism was; from the grainy black-and-white footage shown on TV, it looked like a bleak place where people spent their time making cinder block buildings and standing in line for bread. They also had lots of soldiers, tanks, and the atomic bomb. I had gotten used to hiding under my desk during frequent duck-and-cover drills to prepare for the inevitable air raids that the Communists were waiting to launch.

One of the things Mike Stevenson and I would do to pass the time in the quiet suburbs of La Puente was sit on his roof and listen to FM radio. KPPC was a station out of Pasadena that played the latest rock and folk music. The station had a weak signal, so you needed to sit on the roof to get reception. Programming often included guest speakers who talked about the war. They were rooting for the Communists to win. Now,

I could understand them being against the war, but being for Communism seemed a bit extreme, and I couldn't believe a thoughtful person could want the commies to win.

On the weekends, we would sneak out of our houses and hitchhike to Bond Street in Hollywood. Bond Street had a number of bookstores that specialized in comic books. Mike and I were both collectors at the time, with a special interest in Marvel Comics. On Bond Street, any back issue of *Spider-Man*, *Fantastic Four*, or *Captain America* could be had for the right price. Sometimes we would buy a comic book, but usually we just looked through the store as if we were in the Louvre admiring great works of art. We would examine rare issues in their clear plastic bags as if Michelangelo himself had drawn them.

There were other attractions in Hollywood in 1969. The streets were full of hippies in all sorts of colorful clothes. The women sometimes wore fishnet or see-through blouses, and the men had long hair, just like the protesters did on television. There were head shops selling posters, underground comics, and all sorts of pipes and cigarette papers. There was also the *Los Angeles Free Press*, which I bought as much for its photographs of naked women as I did for the articles it contained, most of which were against the war.

Another thing we liked to do without telling our parents was hitchhike to the love-ins at Griffith Park. We listened to music by Buddy Miles and Country Joe McDonald, and to many speeches against the war. Some of these speeches were made by Communists, but the speakers didn't look like what I thought a Communist should look like. I volunteered at the Green Power Feeds Millions table to make sandwiches out of stale bread and U.S. government surplus peanut butter for the long lines of hungry protesters. I discovered that making sandwiches allowed you to infiltrate the underground. Before long, I was selling the *L.A. Free Press* in my neighborhood until the night I was almost arrested by the West Covina Police for what they called peddling pornography in front of a Denny's restaurant.

The first time I was arrested was that summer in Elysian Park. I was at a concert to promote a national mobilization of antiwar activists to march on Washington, D.C., for another moratorium. The march was sponsored by the Student Mobilization Committee—a front group for several branches of socialist political parties, including a Communist party, the Workers World Party, and its youth wing, Youth Against War and Fascism.

These guys were real, live commies. One Communist I met in the park that day looked very agreeable. She was a young woman wearing a fishnet shirt over a low-riding granny skirt. I was not used to talking to girls who had nipples sticking out of their shirt, and felt a little uncomfortable. Still, I would have done anything she asked. But she only wanted me to help her pass out some leaflets. I would be the best leaflet passer-outer she ever saw, and I would come back for another stack. She would realize that I was a good comrade, and then she would sleep with me in the bushes somewhere.

I never saw her again.

I was passing out leaflets with great gusto when an officer in the Los Angeles Police Department asked me what I was doing. I asked him if he wanted a leaflet. Two officers grabbed me from behind and began to cuff me. They informed me I was under arrest for the distribution of leaflets in a public park. I started yelling about the U.S. Constitution and freedom, and they began to thump me and twist my arms into painful positions. I looked around and saw that there was a lot of thumping going on. We had been surrounded by a thousand LAPD officers wielding nightsticks. They dragged me off toward the pavement where their cruisers were parked, and I could see that several cop cars were damaged, with dents and broken windows. I could smell tear gas.

The cops shoved me into a cruiser and drove up the hill. They had a large staging area set up for booking a mob of people. After being photographed with my arresting officer, who had punched me earlier, I sat handcuffed in a school bus with barred windows and watched the riot unfold on the lawn below. I was fifteen years old. I did not give them my name or any other information, not for legal protection, but because I had not yet figured out what to tell my parents. The cops pegged me as an adult because of my size. So I was on my way to the adult lockup in the old L.A. County Jail, a very famous place, according to my older brother, who was still in there. I was much less afraid of L.A. County Jail than I was of going home, where my stepdad would certainly side with the cops, and maybe even provide some additional thumping.

L.A. County was very educational. I learned if I didn't keep my hands above my head on the wall, I would get a jab of the nightstick. I stood this way for hours while one by one we were booked and locked in our cells. I also learned a lot from the commies. They said that the riot had been staged for the media. The proof was the large staging area where we were booked, which no one had ever seen before, and the fact that the crowd was surrounded and given no way to obey the order to disperse without running a gauntlet of nightstick-wielding cops, or "pigs" as the commies called them.

I had seen this with my own eyes and knew it was true.

Television and newspaper coverage of the riot unanimously blamed the protesters, who were doing nothing more than smoking dope and listening to music, which they had done every Sunday afternoon throughout the whole summer. I missed Monday classes. On Tuesday, the teachers at Bassett High School, where I now attended, would not believe the LAPD had attacked a peaceful crowd with batons. They thought I was crazy.

My stepfather wasn't into my conspiracy theories, either. After bailing me out of county jail—for the third time now—he was sure I was going to wind up in prison like so many of my other relatives. My parents decided it was time to move back to Louisville as soon as my oldest brother got out of L.A. County Jail.

I had left Kentucky a redneck, but I was returning as a full-fledged dope-smoking, vegetarian Communist sympathizer. We moved to Shively, a small community whose claim to fame is that it was the childhood home of Hunter S. Thompson. Shively was in Butler County, of the infamous billboard on the Dixie Highway that said, WELCOME TO KLAN COUNTRY, and featured three hooded Klansmen burning a cross.

Summer was slow in Shively. The only agreeable thing about the area was the willingness of the liquor stores to sell wine to young teenagers. I would take the wine up to my room and drink it while listening to Grateful Dead records. Or I would go across the street and buy large glasses of beer at the softball games behind St. Dennis Church. Eventually I got bored of this and concocted a scheme to get away for a while. There was no place for a commie in St. Dennis. My plan was to convince my mother that I was going to a church-sponsored summer camp for underprivileged children. I had even gotten all the brochures and forms from the church. My mother hated churches, so I was sure she would never check up on it. I had been to such camps before.

After ditching the consent forms in a trash can, I put my thumb out on the Dixie Highway, heading for New Orleans and not having the least idea what I would do when I got there. I had only five dollars in cash for "camp expenses." I arrived on Bourbon Street at midnight. The avenues were full of people, mostly drunken ones. I met a guy selling the local weekly underground paper, the *NOLA Express,* and before long I had my own stack. I started hustling the papers to drunken tourists. Soon I had enough money to buy a gallon of cheap wine. I joined a group of revelers in front of a record store and woke up in a park down by the waterfront.

The first week in New Orleans went by much too quickly, and now it was time to start the hitchhike home. Only a few miles north of New Orleans, I was picked up by a carload of revelers whom I had met on Bourbon Street the night before. They were heading home to Washington, D.C. Thinking I still had a few days, I decided to ride along with them. They dropped me off in Georgetown just past midnight. Again, the streets were filled with hippie tourists smoking pot and drinking wine. Knowing the drill now, I grabbed a stack of the local underground newspapers and proceeded to hawk them as if they contained the only truthful news available anywhere: the true story of the war, the Kennedy and King assassinations, and why the government didn't want us to smoke marijuana. When I had enough money, I bought two quarts of Muscatel wine and hung out in DuPont Circle and slept in the bushes by the highway.

Eventually I made it home. Nobody seemed to notice I had

gone anywhere. But things were different now, and I was planning my escape. I had no wish to go back to high school. I wanted only to hitchhike around the country, selling underground newspapers, looking for the girl with the fishnet shirt. I knew she was out there somewhere.

Instead, I would be enrolling in Butler High School, a new monstrosity built to handle the "white flight" of the people who had moved to Butler County when their neighborhoods were forcibly integrated by the federal courts. The previous year, the National Guard had been called out after the state champion Butler Bears football team had beaten up a group of black students, including a nine-year-old girl. I did not feel welcome in Klan Country.

The first day of school was a fine sunny morning, and I walked to Butler High from our house across the street from the St. Dennis Church. We were on the edge of the district in an old farmhouse, not in the new boxy subdivisions where the white-flighters lived. I was supposed to take the bus, but I had always hated bus rides, especially since I could get there quicker by walking. I was told later that it was forbidden to walk to school, that I must report to the bus driver.

My first-period class was History. When I walked in, the thirty or so students were all deathly quiet. The bell rang, and the eeriness in the classroom grew. A few seconds of this heavy and uncomfortable silence stretched by; then a student got up and headed for the door. Not a word was said, and soon he was followed by another, and then another. Soon the classroom was empty except for three students and the teacher, who, seeing that we weren't moving, left the room himself. I got up to follow, but a voice stopped me.

"Don't follow those rednecks."

The voice came from a tall, thin student with a wispy beard and a spray-painted marijuana leaf on his T-shirt. A pretty girl was sitting in front of him, and she asked me to stay, as well. I stayed. Eventually the students returned, and not another word was said about the whole incident. It was only later, at lunch, talking to my new friends Ed and Becky that I learned what was going on. Ed was from Florida, and Becky was from Ohio, but this was their second year at Butler High.

The walkout had been a planned protest against the court-ordered busing of black students to Butler High. It was the continuation of the violence and harassment of any black student brave enough to board a bus to Klan Country. The first to walk out was the captain of the state-champion Butler Bears football team.

The black students were also aware of the protest, so none of them showed up the first day of school. They were brave, but they weren't crazy. They showed up the next day and were guarded by a phalanx of Butler County police officers. The students walked into the huge building past two thousand white students, took their seats quietly, and unpacked their notebooks and pencils. Afterwards, I followed everybody into the mammoth concrete structure with the long smooth tile hallways. I didn't think anyone was watching me in particular, but the whole atmosphere was still very tense.

As I looked down at the floor, I noticed it had been tiled in mosaic with the image of a large bear's head growling with its teeth bared inside a circle. By the time I had noticed this, I was walking on the bear. I also noticed that everybody else had walked around the bear symbol. I tried to casually step forward, to get off the bear's head, but it was too late. Bobby Joe, the football player from my History class who had been the first to walk out, approached me with a small group of the Butler Bears. They—state champions and saviors of the white race—had been positioned to observe whether any black students would dare walk across the symbol of the mighty team. None had, only me.

I learned later in the day that the black students had known about this tradition, and carefully avoided walking on the bear. One student had faked almost falling into it as if it were a bottomless hole, correcting himself only with great effort. I later found out that was considered a very brave action, and very comical. Even the white students laughed.

No one was laughing when they caught the hippie standing on the Great Seal of the Butler Bears. The laughter didn't start until the thumping had begun, and that lasted until the bell rang that signaled five minutes to get to your first-period class. For most of the football team, including Bobby Joe, that class was History. With a torn shirt, swollen lip, and bruised ego, I took my seat. Ed and Becky gave me looks of encouragement. The Bears were all smiling. I sat and began to plot the capture, torture, and eventual slow death of Bobby Joe and the entire state-champion Butler Bears football team.

Since I was now an official outcast, I hung out with the school's three other hippies and some of the black students under a big oak tree in front of the school. We were scum. Our group now included Brian Chin, who had also skipped the first day, not because he was scared—he held several belts in karate—but because any reason to ditch school was a good one. With few other options for fun, we started a band in Brian's basement and named it after the cheap wine we consumed in large quantities during rehearsals. We were the Boone's Farm Blues Band. I played the harmonica, but not very well. My bandmates just kept my microphone turned down so I could wail away out of key as much as I liked.

My mother was not happy to see her third son becoming a hippie. Halfway through the school year, she tried to put the brakes on it and ordered me to the barbershop. After we exchanged a few angry words, I went up to my room, where my backpack had been packed ever since I returned from my camping trip to New Orleans. With her in hot pursuit and threatening to call the cops, I ran down the street. I beat feet straight to Ed's house and sat there trying to decide what to do.

I heard a rumor that my father, Stewart Lee, was in town. I hadn't seen him since my step-grandfather chased him out of our house with a pistol he kept for that purpose. The last time I saw him, he was running down South Eighth Street toward the bars on Magnolia Street. That was 1966, right before we moved to L.A. Since that time, Stewart Lee had been living with a new wife and kid in Houston.

Stew's mother told me where to find him, in an apartment building near Fourth and Oak, which was pretty much Louisville's skid row. I knew the area.

Ed drove me to the address my grandmother had given me. We climbed three flights of rickety stairs to a shabby rental apartment. There he was, sitting with my two older brothers, Doug and Steve, and Randy Perez, a friend of ours from the old neighborhood in El Monte. They were drinking Fall City Beer. My brother Steve had left home earlier in the year for L.A., where my brother Doug had rented a house. Things had not gone well. They hitched back to Louisville with Randy, a large bearded Angeleno of Mexican descent.

The three moved in with my father, who changed his name to Lee to avoid paying child support for his last child back in

Texas. This dismal scene still seemed better than going back to Butler High School. I settled in, and soon I was out painting houses with my father, my brothers, and Randy Perez when the weather permitted. Randy liked Louisville because no one had ever seen a Mexican before, and he became a celebrity in the dive bars on Fourth Street in no time at all.

Since Stewart Lee's last stint in Louisville, he had adopted the Texas habit of sporting a cowboy hat and a pair of ostrich-hide cowboy boots, something unheard of in Louisville. The regulars at the local bars he frequented started calling him Beef Stew. It fit. He was six foot four, two hundred pounds, and claimed he'd never lost a fight.

On Fourth Street, there was usually a fight every night. My father wasn't in all the fights. Neither were my two older brothers. But I became accustomed to bars erupting in violence and chaos without warning. It was usually over a perceived slight to the honor of the family or, more often, to the honor of Beef Stew's new cowboy hat. He claimed he got both the boots and the hat in Houston off a cowboy after knocking him out in a bar fight. I believed him.

Winter raged on. Snow and rain made it difficult to find work painting houses, which was all that my dad ever did. "Son," he would say, "everything they build has got to be painted. And if they stop building things, then eventually everything will need repainting. I could have been anything I wanted in life, but I chose to be a painter. If you are a good painter, you will never be out of work."

But we were out of work—and broke. In 1970, Louisville was in the midst of a recession that was rapidly turning the industrial heartland into the Rust Belt. Jobs were hard to find, and hundreds of painters were out of work. By April, I had had enough and talked my oldest brother into hitchhiking to Washington, D.C., for the May Day antiwar protest. We made it all the way to Hamilton, Ohio, before we were arrested for hitchhiking. The sheriff's deputy asked us where we were going. We told him.

"Get in," he said. "You ain't going to no protest."

We spent the week in the county jail. I was still a minor, but once again, I was put in the adult jail. We were let out only after the big demonstration was over. We hitchhiked back to Louisville.

Eventually Beef Stew was thinking about his daughter in Texas, the warmer weather, and the demand for good painters. He began to tell us stories of Texas and how we could all get rich if we moved to Houston. He borrowed a hundred dollars from a friend and bought a 1957 Buick Electra with big fins and bald tires. We piled in—Beef Stew, my brothers Doug and Steve, Randy Perez—heading to Houston in the middle of a spring snowstorm. We also had Brian Chin, my friend and bass player in the Boone's Farm Blues Band, and his cousin Carl. They were going all the way to L.A. We arrived in Houston early one morning in the month of May, riding on a flat tire with ice still covering parts of the Buick.

In Houston, Lee—as he was called there—borrowed some more money, and we found an empty apartment where we stayed while he was out looking for work. We were basically squatting in a unit that one of his painter friends was supposed to finish later. Lee took some of the money and rented a Cadillac for a week. Wearing the outfit he took off the unconscious cowboy, which included a nice jacket, he put bids on various painting projects around the city. Before the week was up, Lee was awarded the low bid on a hundred-unit apartment complex.

Owning neither truck nor ladder, just a bucket of brushes and rollers, Lee was undaunted. Next, he went to the paint store, still in his cowboy suit and, after explaining the size of the job, received a line of credit for paint and even ladders. We found an old '52 Chevy pickup, got it running, painted it with a roller, and stenciled, ROSELLE AND SONS: COATING ENGINEERS, on both doors. He rounded up a few unemployed painters from the local bars in the Westheimer District, and we had ourselves a crew. Soon we were rolling in the money.

Lee had a special way of painting apartment units that reduced both the amount of time required and the amount of paint used. First, he would convince the manager that the apartment would need more than just a touch-up, that it would need a complete paint job. Then he would touch it up and charge them for a complete paint job. If they insisted on a touch-up, because the previous tenants had not been in there very long or didn't smoke, or whatever, my father would change the color of the paint by adding white tint, which would make the original color look old and dull. After explaining that he was correct, that it did need a complete paint job, he would touch it up with the correct color. Then charge for both a touch-up and a complete paint job.

If the apartment was a wreck, he could still touch it up, sometimes adding coffee to the paint to make it match the color of nicotine and chicken grease on the walls. It was an art. "The key," Lee would say, "is you got to paint the doors and frames so they can smell paint." Only rarely would we paint an entire apartment. We had the management convinced we were running three crews when the five of us were usually done by noon and were in the Polka Dot playing pool and drinking beer.

It was at this time that my father decided I should go back to school. I was now seventeen years old and had missed a half year of high school. I enrolled in Abraham Lincoln High School in the Westheimer District, which had a student body that was 90 percent African American. I lasted about two weeks. The school was built and operated like a prison. Though my class-mates treated me well, I had little interest in getting a high school diploma. I would rather be working and saving up enough money to get out of Houston and back to California.

One morning, instead of going to school, I hitched out to Los Angeles. I had about ten dollars in cash, which got me as far as El Paso, Texas. There I was picked up by a traveling hip-pie bluegrass band on their way from New Hampshire to Whitethorn, a small town on the coast of northern California. They had no money either, and would stop and play music whenever they needed gas. During these music sessions, I was given a saw and a small hammer. I would strike the hammer on the saw blade while bending it, producing some eerie, if not musical, noises. It took two weeks to reach L.A., and I moved in with Gilbert, a friend of my oldest brother.

Gilbert's house was a refuge for runaways and drug addicts, and a party was usually in progress at all times of the day and night. We lived in Baldwin Park, which bordered La Puente. Because there was not much work, I went back to Bassett High School and enrolled, not bothering to tell them I was no longer living in the district, or with my parents, or with any adults. This worked well for a few weeks until Mr. Krause, the school counselor, saw me walking to school from Baldwin Park, which was outside the school district.

He pulled over and told me to get into the car. I was busted. But I wasn't kicked out of school. I told them the truth about my situation, and they convened a faculty meeting in which they worked out a deal. I would move in with Mrs. Homer, a part-time substitute teacher and mother of one of my class-mates, Mike. I would attend night school to catch up on my classes. They would get me straightened out. I found a week-end job on a construction crew. Eventually Mrs. Homer's house became too much, and I moved back to Gilbert's. No one said anything. I didn't tell anybody at the school. I still walked the two miles to school, but stayed off the main streets to avoid Mr. Krause.

The scene at Gilbert's was getting more and more out of control. He had gotten an inheritance when both his parents were killed in an auto accident. He was addicted to barbitu-rates, and there was a lot of drug dealing going on. One night our house was robbed while we were sleeping. My housemates had eaten all the food I bought for the week. I was spending all my time at either school or my job, and I had very little to show for it. I decided once more to hit the road.

It was 1972, and Richard Nixon was running for his second term as president. Originally, the Republican Convention was going to be held in San Diego, but at the last minute they moved it to Miami, where the Democrats were holding their convention. It was rumored that the change in venue was due to security concerns. There were just too many protesters in California. The hope was that they would not travel the three thousand miles to southern Florida. I decided to hitchhike to Florida for both conventions and left L.A., this time with no money at all.

Interstate 10 ran right by Gilbert's house in Baldwin Park. From there, I made it to San Bernardino, where I got picked up by an aging rock musician in an old Chevy van on his way to

Austin, Texas. Near El Paso he picked up another hitchhiker. It was Aron Kay, whom I had worked with in L.A. at Green Power Feeds Millions, the organization that made the peanut butter–and–jelly sandwiches at Elysian Park. He was on his way to Miami to set up the kitchen for the protesters at both conventions. He stopped in Austin. I went to Houston and worked for Beef Stew, painting apartments until I had a few hundred bucks. Then I, too, set out for Miami.

I arrived in Miami two weeks before the beginning of the Democratic Convention. My first ride in the city was from a man named Red, a tall hippie with long red hair and a beard. He was driving an old Austin Healy sedan. He was on his way to the Coconut Grove section of town, to a house where the Yippies had set up their headquarters. Before he could get there, his car's engine began to overheat. The water pump was leaking badly. Feeling flush with cash, I offered to buy him a used water pump and to put it in if he could get us to a junkyard. This we did without too much effort. When the repairs were complete, he took me to the Yippie house and introduced me to its occupants. The water pump had cost only twenty dollars. It took me a half hour to install, but the pump had been an ongoing problem, and I was now treated as some kind of hero.

If there was a heaven, this is what it should look like. The house was full of activists, all getting ready for the conventions and the big protest marches that were planned. The big issue was the war, but the Yippies were also concerned about gay rights, women's liberation, and legalizing marijuana. But primarily they were concerned with legalizing marijuana, which they smoked in large quantities throughout the day. And there were lots of women.

I was an eager volunteer, and my first assignment was to

finish a papier-mâché sculpture needed for the Smoke-In, a large march and rally to demand the legalization of marijuana. The sculpture was supposed to be in the shape of a thirty-foot-long joint, but was mostly a tangled mess of chicken wire and newspapers. I spent the afternoon straightening chicken wire and applying layer after layer of newspapers soaked in laundry starch. The hot summer sun blazed down in the garden behind the house in Coconut Grove. By evening, the newspapers were dry, and I applied a coat of white house paint. The giant reefer was done. Seeing I had some artistic ability, Dana Beal, one of the head Yippies, asked me to help with the newspaper they were putting out by drawing some graphics.

It had been less than twelve hours since I arrived in Miami, and I was now on the organizing staff for the big demonstrations. I had fixed their car, made a giant marijuana joint, cooked dinner, and helped put the newspaper to bed all in one day. That night I slept on the floor in the office and listened to the sound of people fucking all over the house. Over the next few weeks, I would work during the day with all these liberated women. At night, they would sleep with guys I wouldn't see at all when the work was being done. This seemed unfair, but this place still beat Butler High School, and I still held out a great deal more hope than the situation warranted.

Eventually we moved our whole operation into Flamingo Park, in the heart of Miami Beach, where the city had given the protesters a free place to camp. The largest contingent was the Southern Christian Leadership Conference, the civil rights organization started by Dr. Martin Luther King Jr. It was now led by the Reverend Ralph Abernathy, another hero of the struggle against segregation in the South. There was also a large contingent for Vietnam Veterans Against the War.

The SCLC was camped loosely in a section of the park they called Resurrection City, after the big encampment in Washington, D.C., where Dr. King had delivered his "I Have a Dream" speech. The vets were camped in formation, according to their units or home states, in neat rows with sentries. Flagpoles displayed the unit's colors at the front of each row. There were thousands of them.

Then there were the Students for a Democratic Society. The many hundreds of them all wore the same red T-shirts with a black fist and the word STRIKE! in bold letters. The Gay Activist Alliance was out in force, driven by the spirit of the Stonewall Riots in New York, which had put the issue of gay and lesbian rights on the national agenda for the first time. There were other groups with other acronyms, and I now became aware that there was no Yippie camp. There was no Yippie tent. The Yippies, it turned out, were a tiny fraction of this camp. But they were getting a great deal of media attention due to the still-fresh memory of the brutal riots in Chicago during the last Democratic convention.

Not everybody was happy about this. Being a Yippie was not going to get me laid in this park. I noticed that Green Power Feeds Millions had set up a makeshift kitchen. There was Aron Kay (aka the infamous Pieman), supervising the making of peanut butter–and–jelly sandwiches at a long table with an even longer line. He shook his captive audience down for pocket change by rattling a one-gallon coffee can in front of them. I instinctively took my spot behind the table, making sandwiches. At night, I even slept behind that kitchen table.

The next day, I awoke in the park and it looked like Woodstock. Thousands more people had arrived, and now there were reportedly ten thousand camping in Flamingo Park and ten thousand more spread out in motels and campgrounds in the surrounding area. If any of these people were Yippies, it was very hard to tell. It wasn't long until a bona fide Yippie, Abbie Hoffman, came along to have his picture taken eating a peanut butter sandwich at the Green Power Feeds Millions table. He had been staying at the Doral Hotel in the penthouse. He'd just received a large advance to write a book about the conventions and would be making his first and only foray into the park.

Soon Abbie Hoffman was accosted by a small bookish New Yorker with thick spectacles and long stringy hair. He was A. J. Weberman, who would go on to fame as a "Dylanologist." AJ started going over a long list of crimes against the movement that Abbie had committed. Weberman was yelling in his face when the fight broke out. I didn't see who threw the first punch, but later I learned that AJ had a great talent for getting punched out by the rich and famous. I would guess that Abbie punched him after hearing one of AJ's particularly barbed insults. Before I knew it, I was over the table and had Hoffman by the arms, while Peter, who was also making sandwiches, got in front of AJ.

Abbie Hoffman had been one of my heroes since the eighth grade, and here I was holding him back like some drunk in a bar fight. It wasn't difficult, as he was not a tall person, but he was pretty strong and tried to wiggle free at first. After a few seconds, I let him go.

I was already learning what the fuss was all about. It wasn't just the money, or the media attention that Abbie was getting to the exclusion of everyone else. It was that he disavowed the Yippie movement, saying it had all been just a joke, when thousands of young activists were forming local Yippie chapters in the major cities and college towns across the country.

When asked to address the first national Yippie convention in Madison, Wisconsin, in 1971, Abbie had requested a speaking fee. He endorsed the candidacy of George McGovern without consulting the new grassroots Yippie movement that had sprung up after people started reading his books and taking his advice seriously.

The convention responded to Hoffman's rebuff by changing their name from Yippie to the Zippies. The Zippies hated Hoffman and Jerry Rubin with a vengeance that revolutionaries reserve only for each other. That's why Abbie did not return to Flamingo Park, and it also helps to explain the disorganized state of the Yippie contingent in Miami at the time. Despite all of this, they were receiving a tremendous amount of media attention.

Hoffman quickly left the park with his entourage. Weberman was close on his heels, continuing his stinging indictment at the top of his lungs in hopes that Abbie would punch him again. No one had caught the first punch on camera. Another large meeting was in progress. I walked over to listen in. Few people had paid any attention to the fistfight. They were wrapped up in discussing another issue, the American flag, which was flying high over the park. It was a spirited debate, and many thought the flag should remain. Others thought it should come down. No one could agree on what to replace it with.

For no particular reason, I grabbed a blue-and-red Viet Cong flag from a box of goods behind the Green Power Feeds Millions table. Peter and I went over to the flagpole. I climbed the pole to the cheer of the crowd and replaced Old Glory with the Viet Cong flag, cut the line, and looped the short end around the pole so it could not be lowered from the ground.

As I slid back down, not everyone was cheering. Soon calls

were coming in from all over the country, and it was a big national media story, and the response was all negative. An even bigger meeting was held in the park, and I was held to task. I was made to climb back up and take the Viet Cong flag down. The pole was left empty, and I was now branded by the SDS and SCLC as an agent provocateur. What I did not realize was that for a Yippie this was considered a badge of honor. I finally got laid—for the first time.

That night I was back at the Zippie house, and we stayed up until early in the morning, rolling joints from six pounds of pot Dana had brought down from Madison. The joints were put in small plastic bags, and those were stuck into the belly of the thirty-foot papier-mâché joint, which was now a giant reefer piñata. Later in the day, we paraded it through the streets of Miami, past the convention center, and back to the park where we broke it open for the Smoke-In. There, thousands of people openly smoked marijuana, defying the law. People had been smoking in the park for the last three days, though, so no one really noticed.

The rest of the week was devoted to occupying George McGovern's hotel for a day. We hosted a piss-in, to pee on a pile of books Dana didn't like. We attended and disrupted other demonstrations, and harassed Abbie Hoffman whenever we could find him. The Democratic Convention ended with George McGovern as the nominee. We began to prepare for the renomination of Nixon and his visit to the convention hall to make his acceptance speech.

While the Democratic Convention had been a lovefest with lots of silliness, the Republican Convention would produce a riot almost as big as the one in Chicago in 1968, though more people were arrested in Miami. I hung around the Mary Street house and tried to make myself useful. Bitter divisions were developing among various camps.

The strategy to protest Nixon's speech was simple enough: The dozen or so major intersections around the convention center would be occupied by sit-ins, each one by a different group, in order to disrupt traffic and prevent the Republican delegates from reaching the hall to hear Nixon's speech.

Other groups wanted to use a tactic called "mobile civil disobedience," which meant they would roam the streets in small groups, blocking traffic wherever the feeling struck. This was frowned upon by the main organizers, who thought it would lead to "trashing," or property destruction.

I had joined one of these roving affinity groups. We called ourselves the Godzilla Brigade. At the height of the riot, we were about thirty deep, all wearing red armbands and red T-shirts we had stolen from the Students for a Democratic Society. Some of us were also wearing football helmets, army-surplus gas masks, and flak jackets. It looked pretty radical, but the masks didn't work. You couldn't breathe fresh air, much less the tear gas.

We busied ourselves with pushing Dumpsters into the street and lighting them on fire. At one point, we captured a bus with the prowar South Carolina delegation and forced the terrified conventioneers to walk the several blocks through the chaos to the convention hall in their formal clothes. Angry protesters were pelting them with eggs and pulling on their Nixon buttons. Nixon ended up speaking, but the auditorium was only half-full, and tear gas had gotten into the air-conditioning system. Tears streamed everywhere.

The riot broke out in front of the Doral Hotel, where Nixon was staying and a large group of demonstrators had sat down to block traffic. The initial protest was peaceful and disciplined, led by pacifist and political activist Dave Dellinger. The Miami police nevertheless waded into the crowd and started clubbing people who were offering no resistance. We watched this melee on a television in Flamingo Park. Anger was rising against the police. The protesters had met several times with the cops in an attempt to avoid this kind of spectacle.

A small group started marching around the camp. People began joining in. By the time we left the park to march down Collins Avenue to the Doral Hotel, there must have been two thousand people, already flanked by hundreds of police cruisers. Helicopters hovered in the air above us. We moved down the avenue; all that separated us from the hotel was a canal spanned by a bridge. The cops set up a defensive line at the bridge with an armored military vehicle equipped to shoot pepper spray two hundred feet in any direction. The vehicle was flanked by officers from all corners of Florida wearing full riot gear: helmets, face shields, and nightsticks.

The Miami police were still involved in arresting and clubbing protesters in front of the hotel when they saw this large group of supporters arrive. A loud cheer went up, and the first barrage of rocks and bottles was thrown at the police by specially trained members of the Weather Underground, who wanted the antiwar movement to abandon nonviolence for armed struggle. They appeared out of nowhere. The police struck back with Mace and rubber bullets. Protesters were grabbing the tear gas cans and throwing them back into the police lines. When the police advanced, the perpetrators would fall back and disappear into the crowd, then re-form whenever the police advance had halted.

The battle was no contest. The cops hammered us. We

quickly retreated back down Collins Avenue toward Flamingo Park with the cops in hot pursuit. When we got back to the park, the cops surrounded us and sent in round after round of tear gas. Most people had already left, and the place looked like an abandoned refugee camp. A fellow named Padre and I slipped through the police lines. We made it to the Albion Hotel, where Abbie Hoffman and Jerry Rubin were staying. We walked in wearing our SDS T-shirts and stepped into the elevator. On the second floor, Allen Ginsberg got in the elevator. He immediately recognized us as troublemakers from the park. He said he could smell the tear gas on our shirts.

"You were out trashing, weren't you?" he asked. We said nothing. He gave us a big lecture on how people like us had screwed up everything down here, and that we would get four more years of Nixon because of it. We continued to the top floor, where there was a celebration party for the demonstration's organizers at the penthouse overlooking a pool on the roof of the hotel. We threw Abbie Hoffman into the pool and left.

Afterwards, we grabbed my gear in the park and walked to the Yippie house on Mary Street, using the side streets and alleys to avoid police cruisers, which were everywhere. When we got to the house, the police had just staged a raid. The place had been torn apart and was now empty. I slept there. In the morning, I had little to do, so I started putting the place back together. Over time, some of the Yippies returned, including Red with his Austin Healy, and Rachael, the girl who had stolen my virginity.

The next morning, Red, Rachael, her girlfriends Connie and Katy, Padre, and I set out for East Texas. Red, Padre, and I were heading to Aransas Pass to get jobs on the shrimp boats.

The girls were headed to Dallas to work in a strip club. We got jobs on the boats. I never heard whether the girls were so lucky. After a few months on the boat, I quit in Jacksonville, Florida, where my boat was berthed, and hitchhiked back to California to attend my high school graduation.

I continued working with the Yippies until the inauguration of Richard Nixon in Washington, D.C., which was to be the last large protest against U.S. policy in Vietnam. It would still take a few more years for the war to die down altogether.

When the last troops were pulled out in June 1975, I was listening to news reports on the radio aboard a small sailboat in the Everglades. Both the war and the movement to end it quickly and quietly faded into history. I sat on the bow of the boat with my legs hanging over the sides, staring into the water. I watched the fluorescent glow of the wake as the hull of the boat slipped silently in the light breeze, sailing toward the open sea. For the first time since I'd left home, I had no idea what I wanted to do.

3

Brinkerhoff 54—The Founding of Earth First!

From the derrick, I had a splendid view of the sunrise. I smoked a joint and watched the early light illuminate off a dust cloud kicked up by a herd of horses galloping full speed across the sage-covered hills. I seemed to be living in a Marlboro commercial. Not only that, but I was making a ton of money. It was 1978. Out on Brinkerhoff 54, I had the best job on the newest and biggest rig in Wyoming. The location was perfect, just forty-five minutes from Jackson Hole, a place that would gladly take all your oil field money.

Our location was at the bottom of Granite Creek, which sits on top of the Overthrust Belt, a geological formation that runs from Alberta to New Mexico. The belt is a formation rich in oil, gas, and coal deposits. In western Wyoming, it includes the Frontier Formation, a thick layer of ancient limestone rich in natural gas, and the site of a huge bonanza. In the past, most of this drilling had been to the south of Big Piney. But new discoveries were pushing the oil companies and the drilling rigs north into areas closer to Yellowstone and Grand Teton National Parks.

Not everyone was happy about that. But to most, the encroachment seemed more or less inevitable. I felt okay with my decision to hire on because the driller, Denny Davis, was an old friend and wanted a hand from Jackson, who lived near his house. One who smoked marijuana. One who might know where to get some.

In the 1970s, the Frontier Formation was a driller's paradise. The formation, although rich in natural gas, was broken up into many fragments, turned on its end, and in places folded over on itself. The ridges of these underground nonconformities yielded high-pressure gas, but often it was at a low volume. While some areas of the formation lay only five thousand feet below the surface, in other places its depth exceeded three miles. These variations made the oil fields of Wyoming a regular Las Vegas, with one well producing high volumes of valuable gas and one nearby producing nothing. A labor shortage meant that the drillers were not too picky about whom they hired. I was proof of that.

Originally, I went to the oil fields for the same reason that most of the other roughnecks did. I was broke. I had moved to Jackson from Florida in August of 1975 and found work as a dishwasher, cook, waiter, and maid until the inevitable end of the summer tourist season, when I was laid off. Ski season did not pick up until after Christmas, rent was due on the first, and if I gave the landlord what little money I had, I would probably starve.

In desperation, I decided to try my luck in the oil patch. It was early November and already below zero when I hitched down Highway 89 to Big Piney, a town of five hundred inhabitants at the epicenter of the new oil and gas boom.

I got dropped off at the Silver Spur Bar, which I had heard was the town's unemployment office. Having only enough money for one night in the Country Chalet Motel or to get drunk, I ordered a beer. Before too long, I had met several of the local roughnecks, and just before midnight, a crew leaving the bar was one man short. Denny Davis, the roughneck with whom I'd been drinking, was a driller, and his derrick hand had not shown up. Denny insisted his crew meet him at the bar so he wouldn't have to drive around town and pick everybody up.

He was now impatient. "Grab your rags," he bellowed. "We're going to the rig."

I obliged, and shortly after midnight I was working in the derrick of an oil production rig, a machine I had never even seen before. It looked like a smaller version of a drilling rig mounted on a giant truck, and it was usually used to service the wells after they were drilled. This may sound less glamorous than drilling wildcats, but it's actually much more perilous because the wells are by now pressurized with highly combustible gases and liquids. I was reminded of the dangers by a large black spot on the desert floor not a hundred yards from our rig. We drove by the wreckage of what looked like an antiaircraft battery after being struck by a Cruise missile.

"They hit a high-pressure gas pocket, and it blew eighteen hundred feet of pipe out of the hole like it was spaghetti," Denny said. "A spark hit the derrick leg, and she blew off for two days before the pressure dropped. Pretty much all that was left was a puddle." He related the story as if this sort of event was not an uncommon occurrence. Fortunately no one was hurt, which made me feel a little better. Then I learned that our job was to directionally drill into the same formation because obviously there was going to be some gas down there.

After the first explosion, they set another big rig on the location we were now drilling on. The second attempt produced another disaster, but this time the drill pipe had gotten stuck in the hole. After months of trying to extract it, they sent down an explosive charge and severed it above the spot where it was stuck. The workers pulled up all the pipe except for the drill bit, the drill collars, and a special tool to log the geology of the pay zone.

You'd think that True Oil, the company that owned the lease, would be putting its most advanced equipment on so critical a project. You would be wrong. True 4 had a reputation as one of the most dangerous pieces of junk in the oil patch. It was cobbled together from spare parts and baling wire. The engines belched black smoke, and one of the oil pumps had a length of rope used as a fan belt. The whole time you worked, you were covered in slippery drilling fluids, working on a slippery deck in freezing weather, with the only heat coming from a single forced-air heater, which Denny, weighing in at over 250 pounds, stood in front of. There was no heat in the derrick. Not surprisingly, Denny had gone through more derrick hands than any other driller in the state.

Not that I knew any of the foregoing. Nobody told me, and no one at the Silver Spur thought I'd last very long. But after a few months, I began to enjoy our little rig, liked working with my crew, even though the other roughnecks would tease us about working for the Tonka Drilling Company. By February, I had a wad of cash and had bought an old yellow Ford F-150, so I went back up to Jackson to find a restaurant job. But Denny and I remained friends, and over the years I would return to True 4. Denny was always looking for a derrick hand.

Thanks to my experience with the True Oil Company, eventually I was able to get a position working derricks on a real drilling rig, which paid the most money for the least work. Most days, I would just show up at the rig, sign in, go to the pump house and look at a few pressure gauges and write the numbers in the book. If I was in a hurry, I would just write the numbers down without checking the gauges.

After marking the numbers, I would throw a few sacks of sawdust on one of the big hydraulic pumps in the pump house, right in front of the forced-air heater, and sleep until I heard the pump stop. A pump that stops is about the worst thing that can happen to a derrick hand. It means you have to work, usually by pulling the eight thousand or so feet of pipe out, changing the drill bit, and putting it back in. The procedure could take up to twelve hours and required being in the derrick itself, where there was no heat. It was no wonder derrick hands were hard to find in Wyoming in the winter.

By 1979, I had become a ski bum. Not a downhill ski bum, but a cross-country ski bum—an easier habit to support with my meager finances. A few times a year I would go down to the oil patch and sign on for a month or two. I also worked a few months out of the year in one of the many restaurants in Jackson. Most of the year was spent skiing, hiking, or running rivers, and collecting unemployment checks.

I was working hard on Brinkerhoff 54 at the mouth of Granite Creek when I got the news. Brinkerhoff 54 was brand-new iron, the biggest and the best in Wyoming. It even had a heater in the derrick. I was working hard only because I'd seen the tool pusher, or rig supervisor, pull up to the job site. The best way to look busy when the tool pusher shows up is to grab a bucket of soapy water and scrub the rig. Tool pushers love it when you scrub. He came by and put a huge wad of Redman tobacco in his jaw, which had a pouch the size of a golf ball protruding below his lower lip. He spit a big wad on the floor and offered me a chew.

"Ed, why are you in such a good mood?" I asked. "When we're done here, they will probably send this rig to North Dakota to drill in a frozen cornfield!"

"No way," he answered. "We got a hole not too far from here, just up the canyon, on that saddle right up there," he declared, pointing to a ridge between two snow-covered peaks in the proposed Gros Ventre Wilderness.

"Aren't the local tree huggers up in arms about that area?" I asked the crusty old pusher, trying not to give away the fact that I was one of those "radicals."

"Doesn't matter. We've got the paperwork," he growled. "It's Getty Oil, and we signed the contract last year. There is a year-long waiting list for drill rigs here in the Overthrust. They need to be ready to spud as soon as we reach bottom rig. Or go shopping for another rig."

I was now presented with a dilemma. For the past few years, I had been supporting efforts by local environmentalists to keep oil and gas development out of Teton County. I was not against drilling for oil. But I had become convinced that drilling had its limits. Those limits included no drilling in roadless areas.

One thing was certain: If Rig 54 was moving into the proposed Gros Ventre Wilderness, I would not be moving with it. I had to tell someone about the plans. And I knew the perfect guy.

Back in Jackson, I gave this news of our new location to Howie Wolke, the most visible wilderness advocate in the region and the most vocal opponent of drilling in the Gros Ventre.

I met Howie when I first came to Jackson while we were both working in the same restaurant. With a large beard, long hair, plaid shirt, and floppy felt hat, he looked more like a logger than like a college graduate from New Hampshire. Only he was bigger and stronger than most of the loggers I'd met.

I got to know Howie just before I went down to the oil fields, and we remained friends even while I was working for the enemy. Howie, too, had worked in the oil patch, as had just about every young male who lived in Wyoming at that time. Howie introduced me to Bart Koehler, who was an organizer for the Wilderness Society, based in Cheyenne. He was a lead opponent of oil and gas exploration and development in the region. Bart, a stocky man with a bushy mustache, always sported a Stetson and wore cowboy boots, even though he was from upstate New York and hated cows.

Howie was not surprised to hear about the contract, but the Environmental Analysis was not out yet, and the decision was not supposed to be final until after its release. More than anyone, Howie had fought the Forest Service's plan to lease the area, and had organized considerable opposition in Jackson, which now included the Sierra Club, the Wilderness Society, and a number of smaller local groups.

Originally, Getty had planned two wells, one in the popular Cache Creek drainage just outside of town, where many of the townspeople jogged, walked their dogs, and rode their horses. Cache Creek would rally so much opposition that the Forest Service decided to first go for the Little Granite

Creek lease, which was not so familiar a place to residents of Jackson.

Howie and I attended a meeting. The most vocal opponents were there. We were not invited to the meeting, because Howie's position was already well known. But naturally, we went anyway. Many of the local conservationists felt that since this was the first time anyone had opposed an oil well on federal land in Wyoming, it would be best to focus on the one that had the most opposition. Howie argued that from a wildlife and wilderness perspective, Little Granite was much more important than Cache Creek. Only by browbeating the local conservationists—specifically the Jackson Hole Conservation Alliance—was Howie able to get them to agree to fight both leases.

"We need to fight both the wells," Howie argued. "If we just stop the Cache Creek well and allow them to build a road into Little Granite Creek, in the heart of the Gros Ventre, then they can come into Cache Creek from above, without bringing their equipment through town, and there will be little we can do about it, because the Gros Ventre will no longer be wilderness, but an industrial oil field."

Howie's plea had hit its mark. After a brief and uncomfortable silence, Dr. McCloud, a local MD who had delivered some of the people in the room, stood up to speak. At eighty years of age, he was a man who commanded respect from everyone present.

"Howie is right. I say we fight both of them. If we win in Cache Creek and lose in Little Granite Creek, we will have lost the Gros Ventre," McCloud said. Silence followed as this assertion sank in. And then all agreed that both decisions would be appealed. Jackson conservationists were now committed to oppose all oil exploration in the proposed Gros Ventre wilderness. There would be a fight!

By now, I was beginning to wonder about the people I was working with. I was used to working with anarchists and hippies, and I was the only hippie in the room. Or so I thought. While most of the people in the room fit the stereotype of a conservationist, Howie was different. He was part of a new breed of conservationist. These were Buckaroos.

From what I could gather, being a Buckaroo meant being an organizer in the fight to protect wilderness, and the head Buckaroo was a fellow named Ken Sleight in Moab, Utah. Ken was the inspiration for the character Seldom Seen Smith in Edward Abbey's novel *The Monkey Wrench Gang*, which was required reading for all Buckaroos, along with Aldo Leopold's *A Sand County Almanac*, and of course, Henry David Thoreau. Wilderness, for a Buckaroo, was the only reason for living, other than alcohol and sex. The former they consumed in large quantities, and the latter they discussed endlessly.

At least, this was my impression after meeting these men. There were female Buckaroos, for sure. Among them, Louisa Willcox and Susan Morgan, Karen Tanner, Sharon Netherton, and many others, no less tough than the men. Phil Hocker, Bruce Hamilton, Andy Kerr, and a host of other men were also Buckaroos, if somewhat more sober ones. This Wyoming Buckaroo behavior was at odds with everything I had been taught about organizing.

One of the honcho Buckaroos was Dave Foreman, a muscled, wiry man from New Mexico with a beard and droopy mustache that ended below a less-than-generous chin. Howie, Bart, and Dave were the most notorious of the bunch. But the women, who were more typically progressive and level-headed, did not seem to take these cartoonish characters too seriously. Together they made up the advance guard of the wilderness movement. Most of them were professionals. Bart and Dave worked for the Wilderness Society, one of the oldest and most respected organizations in the country. Howie had recently quit his job with Friends of the Earth after serving from 1976 to 1979. There were Buckaroos who worked for the Sierra Club and the Audubon Society. Others were volunteers or leaders of smaller groups. The Buckaroo ranks seemed large.

I was not a Buckaroo. My crew in Jackson was a small group of avid cross-country skiers and mountain climbers. Howie Wolke was among them, and from the beginning he was always attempting to enlist us in one of the campaigns he was organizing. In this way, I slowly became active in the local environmental movement and began to learn about what was going on around me.

And there was a lot going on. We were in the midst of a great land rush, spurred on by John Denver's song "Rocky Mountain High" and the rising popularity of winter sports like downhill skiing and snowmobiling. All this love was threatening to destroy the place, or at least that's what I had thought. And I had rather mixed feelings because I was, of course, part of the problem—wasn't I?

Not according to Howie. "The real problem is that there are just too many fucking people on this planet, period!" he related to me on the occasion of our first backcountry ski trip in the Grand Tetons. "The other problem," he continued, "is that there's just not enough wilderness. And it's the timber, mining, and oil companies that are doing the most damage. There aren't enough people fighting for wilderness, Mike. They all come up here to enjoy it, to buy a piece of it, build a house, and they won't lift a finger to protect or defend it."

So Howie *wasn't* talking to me, right? But noticing the way he was glaring at me, I was not so sure. I had no children and owned no property. But up until then I had done little or nothing other than ski, hike, climb, and get drunk since I'd pulled into town. Soon enough, I was accompanying Howie to public hearings, slide shows, mailing parties, and meetings, places where Buckaroos were sure to be hanging out. I was always ready for the work to be done so we could find the nearest bar and the drinking could begin. Buckaroos were not afraid to drink in logger or oil-worker bars. They were not afraid to argue with the loggers and roughnecks. They especially liked to tell the Forest Service employees what was on their minds. In the bar is where the Buckaroos were made. Here, I served my apprenticeship more or less successfully. Soon, I was invited to go on a Buckaroo trip to Mexico.

The year before, Howie, Dave Foreman, and Bart Koehler had gone to Mexico to eat shrimp, drink, and be merry. I spoke to Howie about it after he returned, and he had many stories. Some of the stories I would hear many times—mostly stories about deserts, bars, and hookers.

This year they were going to the Pinacate Natural Park in northern Sonora, just across the Arizona border. In the spring of 1980, Howie and I drove down to Rock Springs, Wyoming, where we met Bart and took the Greyhound bus down to Tucson, Arizona, and met Dave Foreman and Ron Kezar, a Sierra Clubber living in El Paso, Texas. According to Foreman, Kezar was a little crazy, and I never saw a reason to doubt him. He had an eerie smile and a way of looking at you as if he were curious about the best method to dismember your body and hide the evidence.

From Tucson, we crossed the border, bought some beer, and headed for Pinacate Peak, a large cinder cone rising in the center of a gigantic lava flow that spread out on the hot desert, making it look even more hellish. By late afternoon we had scaled the peak, and we returned to our camp and consumed copious amounts of alcohol until late in the evening, when we were literally howling at the moon.

By this time, I could discern the true reason for the Buckaroos' sad lament. The story begins with the passage of the Wilderness Act, which created a new form of protection for public lands in the United States. The act was a monumental piece of legislation originally championed by conservationists like Aldo Leopold and Bob Marshall. Later Howard Zahniser, executive director of the Wilderness Society, was the author and visionary who pushed the bill through Congress, though Zahniser died shortly before it was signed into law by Lyndon Johnson on September 3, 1964.

The Wilderness Act immediately classified 9.3 million acres of national forest land as designated wilderness, and required the federal government to create a public process to determine which areas should be protected in the National Wilderness Preservation System. The act gave the Secretary of Agriculture ten years to study the suitability of thirty-four national forest areas classified as "primitive." But it gave no direction to the Forest Service as far as how to manage roadless areas that were not already classified as primitive areas.

In response to public demand, the Forest Service began its first inventory of all roadless areas in the national forest in 1972. The process was called RARE, or the Roadless Area Re-

view and Evaluation. It would take an inventory of every national forest roadless area in the United States, over 5,000
acres, and recommend those deemed most suitable for protection.

RARE set off a scramble of near biblical proportions. Oil,
gas, and timber interests quickly depicted RARE as an unprecedented land grab by the federal government. Wait a minute—
weren't these lands already owned by the federal government?
Conservationists hailed RARE as the last best chance for some
of the nation's most threatened wilderness areas. To meet this
challenge, the big environmental groups, led by the Wilderness
Society, launched a major grassroots campaign. They hired a
staff of organizers who knew and worked in the West to run the
campaign, since many of the most contested areas were located
there.

The first RARE effort concluded in October of 1973 with
the selection of 274 wilderness study areas containing about
12.3 million acres. Those selections were made from a total
inventory of 1,449 areas containing 56 million acres. Less than
a quarter of the remaining roadless land would be protected.

The environmental movement was outraged. I mean *pissed*.
There was a major lawsuit by the Sierra Club, and the controversy escalated.

In 1978, RARE II was announced by Carter administration
Assistant Secretary of Agriculture Rupert Cutler, a former employee of the Wilderness Society. The U.S. Forest Service went
back to the drawing board and began RARE II, which was essentially a rematch.

A rematch is not the same as a win. From the green sidelines,
there was still no way to stop the oil, gas, mining, ranching,
and timber industries from liquidating the last best places.

Except now, the extractive industries were picking up the pace. The big-name environmental groups were starting to back off a full-protection stance, so as not to alienate their "friends" in the Carter administration. Meanwhile industry groups would support protection only for rocks, ice, and lava flows—any place the ground was absent oil, gas, timber, or minerals to exploit.

RARE II was debatably more ambitious than RARE I. And now the public was paying attention. The industry kicked up a multimillion-dollar campaign, and the conservationists geared up for another big fight. Before going in, they wanted unity among all the allied groups. A compromise was reached by an assembly of all the big groups. It was called Alternative W, which proposed about one half the acreage in question for wilderness designation.

From the beginning it was a hard sell. These lands were in the care of the federal government, and were to be maintained for the benefit of all Americans, and indeed the whole world.

Organizing in the West was not an easy assignment, and these field organizers learned the hard way that outsiders would not be welcomed by the locals, much less be seen as credible advocates. On the contrary, the industry had succeeded in branding them as dangerous radicals. A small percentage of the locals were downright hostile, and their embers of rage were fanned by the timber industry into outright fiery violence.

Reason held no sway under such circumstances, and there was no way to convince many of the locals that wilderness had any real value, even though a majority of them dreaded seeing the West they loved plundered by logging, mining, and oil drilling. They were convinced wilderness designation would cause the area to be overrun with hippie backpackers from

California who spent very little money in the region because they lived on a steady diet of granola. No matter how hard the Buckaroos tried, they could not convince the majority of locals that wilderness designation would actually preserve the status quo by limiting the scope of large industrial development on the public domain.

Seeming to condone this atmosphere of fear and intimidation, the U.S. Forest Service made sure to schedule the public hearings on RARE II in small timber-dependent communities like Dillon, Montana; Dubois, Wyoming; Forks, Washington; Sweet Home, Oregon; and anywhere else that conservationists expect to be outnumbered ten-to-one by timber-industry supporters, many of whom received wages for attending those hearings.

There were more than a few cases where witnesses testifying in favor of wilderness in some of these towns had to exit quietly through the back door. The RARE II field organizers had learned to be brave and tough. They confused the locals, wearing cowboy attire to blend in better.

A true Buckaroo could be distinguished by his or her clothes: Wranglers, boots, a cowboy shirt, and a hat. On their frequent trips to Washington, D.C., to meet with bosses and colleagues, the Buckaroos stood out from the suits and ties cloistered in the nation's capital. Buckaroos wore their cowboy clothes as if they were a badge of honor. And indeed, they were.

Try as they did, the conservationists were headed toward defeat. RARE II was completed in January of 1979 and identified 2,919 roadless areas that contained a little more than 62 million acres. The Forest Service recommendation was for over half that land, 36 million acres, to be allocated for nonwilderness uses, like logging, mining, and oil drilling. About a quarter of the land, 15 million acres, would be recommended for addition to the National Wilderness Preservation System. Another 11 million acres would be placed into another category known as "Further Planning" and would be decided on after more study.

On the surface, things didn't look that bad for conservationists, but if you peered a little deeper, the process that was supposed to protect wilderness was excluding three quarters of national forest roadless areas, while over half was being released for development in one fell swoop. The half-assed Alternative W strategy had backfired, and now there were no protections or avenues to stop the wholesale destruction of the almost forty million acres of pristine de facto wilderness, while another 11 million acres were held in limbo, without any real protection.

The meager recommended numbers for roadless habitat protection reflected the antiwilderness bias of the Forest Service bureaucracy. Then Congress got a hold of it. The result was that each state would be left to sort it out with individual wilderness bills that had to be introduced by the state's congressional delegation. Since in many western states, these delegations were hostile to the whole idea of wilderness preservation, it meant few wilderness bills would ever see the light of day.

"Alternative W was a wimpy strategy," grumbled Foreman as he took a deep drink from a bottle of cheap mescal. "We should not only have asked for everything, we should have demanded that they remove roads in areas where they never should have been built in the first place." Howie and Bart nodded in agreement. Howie had pushed Friends of the Earth into breaking ranks with the other big groups and advocating for more protection in Wyoming than offered by Alternative W.

We made it into sleeping bags just as dawn began to light up the eastern horizon, and woke up soon afterwards when the full blaze of the sun made the desert floor too hot for sleeping. Before returning home, there was one more stop, the Zona Roja, or red-light district of San Luis. Kezar had heard from knowledgeable sources that this was the right place for a Buckaroo to wash down some of the trail dust and have a few laughs. Yeah, right.

San Luis's modest Zona Roja was situated next to a garbage dump and had clearly seen better days. Half the establishments were closed and boarded up. The two that were open were busy, full of American military men, groups of Chicanos from Arizona, and a number of locals, some sitting with women, and everybody enjoying the floor show. When we entered, the show consisted of a magician who told jokes.

There were also singers, dancers, and a stripper who was clearly not into her job. There were a few sad-eyed women pretending to move with the music, which came from a very bad band that looked to be composed of local teenagers. Sitting at the table with the Buckaroos, I waited as they made up their minds and disappeared out the rear door, only to reappear a few short moments later two hundred pesos lighter.

Hearing about the nature of these brief encounters at the table, it hardly seemed like much fun. I wasn't looking forward to the moment when it was my turn. I developed a strategy that I thought would impress the Buckaroos and preserve my integrity. I simply went out the back door with a woman who was not having much luck with the soldiers—even the really drunk ones—paid her, and waited for a few minutes while we chatted in her very limited English. She seemed to understand what was going on, even if the unsuspecting Buckaroos didn't. When

I returned to the table, triumphant with my consort, the Buckaroos responded with a chorus of hooting and hollering, and
inducted me into their ranks.

I felt honored, but was not quite sure I deserved it.

We woke up at the dump, where we had made a dry camp
after leaving the club, and we all had tremendous hangovers,
empty wallets, and perhaps some feelings of remorse. The
whole thing was soon forgotten, as we headed back to Albuquerque in Foreman's VW van.

First, we dropped Bart off in Tucson to pursue a love interest he had met on the bus ride down from Wyoming. We
dropped Kezar off in Glenwood, New Mexico, to tend to his
crops. Dave, Howie, and I drove on toward Albuquerque. During this drive, Dave and Howie became excited while listing a
comprehensive system of huge multimillion-acre wilderness
preserves that they thought the conservation movement should
promote, instead of wimpy proposals such as Alternative W.
They were drinking beer from cans and tossing them out the
window with a shout of "Hayduke lives!" in honor of Edward
Abbey's eco-saboteur character in his novel *The Monkey Wrench
Gang.*

Soon they decided they couldn't rely on the Sierra Club or
the Wilderness Society to advocate wilderness on such a grand
scale, so it was time to form a new organization. Howie pulled
out some typing paper, and he and Dave started listing the
platform for the new group somebody should start. The first
part of the platform was a system of ecological preserves in
every major eco-region of the United States. They were against
anything that threatened biodiversity.

Then came the bullet points. All the points ended in the
word *period*. For instance,

No strip mines, period.
No nukes, period.
No logging in roadless areas, period.

After a while, they had filled two sheets of paper with bullet points and periods and the words, "No compromise," written out in between.

The next issue was the name. There were several suggestions, including Biological Diversity First, which didn't really roll off the tongue. There were other combinations of our favorite words—Defend Mother Earth, Earth Defense, and such—but nothing was sticking.

Howie said that the group's logo should be a green fist, because that would keep us from ever selling out. It was Foreman who uttered the words "Earth First" after some other suggestions. Using a Bic pen, I took the new platform and sketched in a crudely drawn fist and assembled the characters for EARTH FIRST around it in blocky capital letters. I showed the results to Dave and Howie.

"It needs an exclamation point," Foreman advised. One was added. We now had just about everything a new group needed, except the group. In Albuquerque, after eating one of Dave's mom's renowned chicken-fried steak dinners, Foreman dropped Howie and me off at the Greyhound bus station, where we took the bus back to Rock Springs, picked up Howie's car, and drove the rest of the way to Jackson.

And that was about it. A drunken trip to Mexico, followed by a few hours of drunken brainstorming, a few pieces of paper, and I was back in my house in Moose, Wyoming, looking for a job. I found one working for an Oklahoman who was opening a new barbecue restaurant a block off the town square.

Soon, Bart Koehler came back to Jackson and needed a place to stay. Bart had recently quit his job at the Wilderness Society quite dramatically.

After a hearing in Pinedale, Howie, Bart, and I accompanied *Casper Star-Tribune* reporter Warren Wilson to the bar. After a few drinks, Bart started ranting and raving about William Turnage, the new executive director for the Wilderness Society. Bart told the press that Turnage was a fund-raiser and compromiser, not an organizer, and that he was turning the society into a D.C. think tank. Under executive director Stewart Brandborg and national field director Clif Merrit, the Wilderness Society had been a grassroots-organizing powerhouse. Under Turnage it certainly didn't resemble the organization started by Bob Marshall and Aldo Leopold.

"I'm mad as hell and I'm not gonna take it anymore," Bart said. "I quit."

Warren kept responding to Bart's barrage of quotes with the statement, "Bart, are you sure you want to say that?"

Sure enough, the next day Bart's resignation was on the cover of the paper, along with a string of colorful comments about Turnage.

Despite RARE II, the Forest Service pursued a way to settle the wilderness issue once and for all—build roads into every area that was not yet protected. The Forest Service were doing this with great vigor, and no project proposed by big industry was considered too big, too polluting, or too destructive.

There were new logging roads linking the Upper Green River Basin with the sawmills in Dubois (pronounced *DOO-boyz*) that cut through the heart of the wilderness and would open up the northern part of the Wind River Range to extensive clear-cutting.

There were new uranium mines proposed for the Red Desert, oil shale in Utah, oil and gas everywhere, along with an expansion of the timber industry. Paycheck or no paycheck, both Bart and Howie were not prepared to give up the fight.

Bart also had another reason for being in Jackson; he was the advance committee for the Round River Rendezvous, another idea of Foreman's. It was to be a big wilderness summit, and all the Buckaroos were invited.

Foreman had mentioned his plans for the Round River Rendezvous during our trip to Mexico. It was named for Aldo Leopold's essay, "Round River," and the drunken wilderness soirées of the frontier fur trappers. His reasoning was that part of the problem was that many of the people in the wilderness movement had not actually seen much wilderness, and it was much easier to compromise on a place you'd never been to. By having more meetings in the wild, and having discussions around a campfire like John Muir, Aldo Leopold, and David Brower had done, much more could be accomplished than could be done at a meeting in Washington, D.C., or San Francisco. In fact, many activists had never really met, and knew each other mostly from letters and phone calls and from attending short meetings.

The Round River Rendezvous would bring together the best minds for a week of hiking, drinking, and carousing. Foreman advertised it this way in the invitation: "Get Drunk, Get Laid, and Get Beat Up by Howie Wolke." He was mostly kidding, and soon had to apologize for his comments. But the date had been set, and it was now up to Bart to secure a location, which he did, at the T-Cross Ranch north of Dubois near Yellowstone.

As a newly minted Buckaroo, I found my role in all of this,

even though I was in no sense an organizer, policy expert, researcher, writer, or anything else. I was a cook at a local restaurant. "No problem," Foreman said. "You can do the barbecue."

The Rendezvous was held over the July Fourth holiday and attended by about seventy people, all activists, and a few from the big cities. Around the campfire, Foreman read the Earth First! manifesto and explained why it was now necessary.

"We are getting killed out here in the western states because we are seen as weak, effete, and wimpy. When we cozy up to our friends in Congress, we are co-opted, we are told to be reasonable, we are told to be patient," Foreman said. "We need to be more visible, more confrontational, and I think we should take a lesson from the civil rights movement and use civil disobedience. When they try to build these new roads, we should try to block them!" There was a round of applause, and more drinking. By this time, half the crowd was probably thinking Dave, Bart, and Howie had gone nuts. The rest became converts.

Afterwards, there was a solemn ceremony where Dave, Bart, and several other former Wilderness Society field organizers who also had recently quit, burned their Wilderness Society Patches in the fire. The mood was gloomy. Jimmy Carter, an avowed environmentalist, had released more wilderness to development, via RARE II, than his Republican predecessors had done in the previous twelve years.

Foreman was right: A new wilderness movement was necessary. The old days when you could buttonhole a few machine politicians and convince them to sponsor a conservation bill against local opposition were over. Western states wanted more power over federal lands.

The industry-funded Sagebrush Rebellion had given rise to

new grassroots opposition against environmental regulation threatening to overturn federal legislation like the Endangered Species Act. The Iran hostage crisis further weakened Jimmy Carter, and the Republicans were threatening to return to the White House and undo more than one hundred years of hard-won progress in protecting federally owned lands.

In late April 1980, Earth First! staged its debut action in New Mexico. Foreman, a few friends, and the "masked mason" erected a crude stone monument to Gregorio, an Apache who led a raid on a mining camp on April 28, 1880, possibly the first recorded anti-mining protest in U.S. history. Other than a small article in the weekly Silver City newspaper, the action went largely unnoticed.

On January 20, 1981, the first Earth First! meeting was held in the home of Susan Morgan in Breckenridge, Colorado. Howie and I had driven down from Jackson for the meeting and warned Susan that we would need to wrap up the meeting by four o'clock so we could go find a bar and watch the game. Sure enough, the meeting was still going when Howie and I rose to leave.

"Where are you guys going?" asked Susan.

"To the bar," replied Howie. "The game is about to start."

"What game?" Susan asked.

Evidently, she thought we were joking, as did a number of others present, but we went down to the bar and watched the Super Bowl. We cheered for the Raiders, and Oakland beat Philly. By then, we had already agreed that our next action would be in March at the Glen Canyon Dam in Arizona.

The Glen Canyon Dam is a symbol to many conservationists of what happens when you try to reach a compromise on gigantic environmentally destructive projects. The Bureau of

Reclamation had planned to build a total of fourteen large dams along the Colorado River, including two in the Grand Canyon, one above at Marble Canyon and one below, at Bridge Canyon, and also at Echo Park in Dinosaur National Monument.

The struggle to save the Colorado River started in 1949, when the Colorado River Storage Project was first proposed. Controversy against the project went on for nearly seven years. The battle gave birth to the modern environmental movement, and during the course of the campaign, the Sierra Club was transformed by its charismatic leader, David Brower, from an outdoor hiking club into a powerful political pressure group. As the club took on these new battles, its membership and its reputation reached new heights.

As the 1950s progressed, some environmental leaders became fearful of appearing too extreme. They figured that opposing all the dams would backfire politically. They agreed to withdraw their opposition to the Glen Canyon Dam and to the Colorado River Storage Project, as long as the Grand Canyon dams and Echo and Split Mountain dams were left out of the plan. There was also an agreement that the waters of Powell Reservoir would not flood Rainbow Bridge National Monument.

The CRSP passed in April of 1956. On October 15, 1956, Glen Canyon Dam construction began. It took another fourteen years for Lake Powell to completely submerge almost two hundred miles of pristine canyon wilderness that some visitors said surpassed even the Grand Canyon itself in beauty and grandeur.

Brower would later refer to his decision to withdraw his opposition to the Glen Canyon Dam as the biggest mistake of his life, and became convinced that no one should ever agree to trade off a place where they had never set foot. Compromise was not the job of the conservation groups, he argued. There are plenty of politicians around who want to do that. Brower was too hard on himself. Most likely it was beyond his control to stop any dam from being constructed on the Colorado River, but at least he stopped a few. Nevertheless, the loss of Glen Canyon remains a graphic symbol of the cost of compromise.

Brower was later forced out of the Sierra Club and founded Friends of the Earth. He stated that the conservation movement needed a group that would make the Sierra Club look moderate, one that wouldn't compromise ideals for the sake of appearing reasonable. Friends of the Earth more or less fulfilled that role for a few years.

One of the Glen Canyon Dam's other vocal critics was author Edward Abbey. His novel, *The Monkey Wrench Gang*, about a band of eco-saboteurs planning to blow up the Glen Canyon Dam, had developed almost a cult following among environmental activists and had inspired intense hatred of what Abbey referred to as "the monstrosity."

It was only natural to ask Abbey to appear at the Glen Canyon Dam Earth First! protest. Foreman wrote Abbey a letter requesting his presence at the event. In light of the famous writer's reputation for being cantankerous and antisocial, Foreman was unsure how the man would respond. To Foreman's delight, Abbey readily agreed to speak and sent Dave a two-hundred-dollar check to cover "expenses."

Abbey indeed arrived, and even a few days early, along with his wife, Clark. A group of about fifty Earth Firsters had gathered at the campground in Lone Rock, on the Arizona side of Lake Powell, and the two mingled easily with the activists assembled around the campfire.

A film crew had shown up the day before, expecting to interview Abbey, but they had aroused suspicion due to the large cache of sophisticated electronic equipment in their van. Foreman thought they might be cops.

Bart, Howie, Dave, and I, attired appropriately, ambled cowboy-style over to their campsite and began to interrogate the three California filmmakers: Randy Hayes, Toby McCloud, and Glen Switkes. Sensing danger, Switkes immediately offered up a quart of homebrew he had made himself. He explained that they had been begging Abbey for an interview without success for some time. Finally Abbey agreed. He told them to meet him at Lone Rock, "where something would be going on."

After a few quarts of homebrew took effect, we welcomed the filmmakers into our confidence. Earth First! would be hanging a mock crack on the dam during the protest rally. The crack was made of two hundred feet of black vinyl that we would unfurl down the front of the dam. The filmmakers decided to stick around for the action and agreed to record the stunt two days later.

The first action went off without a hitch. Expecting the worst, the dam's security was positioned in the bowels of the structure. The team of five dam crackers simply walked out on the dam and unfurled the plastic crack supported by rope and duct tape. There were no arrests, and Earth First! received mention in the Denver daily *Rocky Mountain News*. This was our first real coverage. Foreman and Koehler teamed up for a series of road shows, with Koehler performing environmentally themed folk songs under the name Johnny Sagebrush. The act was a hit with audiences, and the duo were able to keep the fledgling organization afloat by passing the hat and selling bumper stickers, T-shirts, and subscriptions to the *Earth First! Journal*—now the voice of a new movement.

Ronald Reagan was now president, and he appointed James Watt as his Secretary of Interior. Watt was perhaps the most polarizing Interior Secretary in history, and his industry-friendly policies were galvanizing public opposition in a way never seen before. After the rendezvous, Earth First! held a protest vilifying Watt in Arches National Park that was attended by a hundred people. Ed Abbey was again the speaker. Life was good for Earth First!

A raucous protest at the Western Governor's Conference held in Jackson that year garnered us our first national television news story when Howie slipped through Watt's security and confronted the secretary face-to-face. "I'm Howie Wolke." He grinned as he firmly held Watt's weak and sweaty hand in a prolonged handshake. "I organized this demonstration, and we're going to stop your destructive policies!"

In July 1981, the second Round River Rendezvous was held on the banks of the Green River just outside Moab, Utah. The gathering was about the same size as the year before, but not everyone had returned, and there were lots of new people.

Foreman and Koehler continued their road show. New groups were formed, and more stories were appearing in newspapers and magazines about the new radical environmental movement. The 1983 Round River Rendezvous was planned for an area adjacent to the proposed Gros Ventre Wilderness near Jackson, Wyoming. It was set against the backdrop of the proposed Getty Oil Company exploratory well in Little Granite Creek. I still worked on the rig—Brinkerhoff 54, our shiny new drilling rig, the biggest and the best rig in the whole state.

Already, largely thanks to the efforts of Howie and Bart and the other Wyoming activists, the public hearings were packed with people angrily denouncing the plans to put an oil field in roadless country so close to Grand Teton National Park. Polls showed that over 90 percent of Teton County residents opposed the idea, but the Forest Service refused to back off, and had already sold the lease.

Abbey wrote to an environmental ethics professor in Georgia in 1982 responding to criticism of *The Monkey Wrench Gang*. Abbey said *The Monkey Wrench Gang* was a fictional comedy. In real life, civil disobedience works best, Abbey said.

"When and if the Getty Oil Co. attempts to invade the Gros Ventre wilderness (Wyoming) with bulldozers, we intend to peaceably assemble and block the invasion with guitars, American flags, live human bodies, and maybe an opposing D-9 tractor," Abbey wrote. "If arrested, we shall go to jail, pay the fines and try again. We invite your readers to join us. A good time will be had by all."

When the snow began to melt in late June 1983 in the high country of Little Granite Creek, the surveyors began their work plunging survey stakes into the earth, marking the path of the road to the drill site on a mountain saddle. They had finished surveying half the seven-mile road when Howie drove up to the trailhead, pulled out all the stakes, and hid them in the woods.

The surveyors pressed on, restaked the lower road, and were almost to the saddle when Dave Foreman, Bart Koehler, and I surprised them while they were eating lunch under a tree. We waved, and on the walk back to the VW van, we pulled up every survey stake all the way down to the Granite Creek trailhead. We were within sight of good old Brinkerhoff 54.

We piled into Foreman's VW van. He was wearing a camouflage T-shirt and a fluorescent orange length of survey tape as a headband. Almost immediately, we encountered the angry surveyors, who pulled their truck alongside the van.

This being no time for polite conservation, we ignored them and set off down the road with the surveyors in hot pursuit. We were headed toward Dog Creek, where my landlord, Paul Gilroy, was hosting a barbecue, which he called Beer, Bear, and Beans. This was a big local get-together, and all of Jackson society would be his guests. Gilroy was also a plaintiff in our lawsuit against Getty Oil. Paul didn't really care about oil drilling in other locations.

Gilroy had a hunting camp in Little Granite Creek that would be worthless if a road went in. The Dog Creek Ranch was just off the road to Alpine, west of Hoback Junction. We were only a few miles from the party. The Dog Creek turnoff disappeared in a thicket of willows and aspen, and if we could get there, we could disappear in the thick brush.

The surveyors did not give up. They followed us to the junction and stopped at the phone booth to call the police. This gave us just enough time to take the turn and disappear up Dog Creek, where most of the cops would be anyway. We pulled into Gilroy's and piled out of the VW van, all of us sporting Day-Glo orange survey tape headbands. We went straight to the keg, and there encountered the great bear hunter.

"I was going to ask you where you fellers had been," Paul

said, "but looking at ya now, I'm guessing I don't want to know."

"We just went up to the wellhead to look around to see if there were any surveyors," I offered.

"See any?" he asked.

"They were right behind us. I was guessing you had invited them up here to the party," I said.

The next day, Howie, Dave, and I had an appointment with the recreation officer for the Bridger Teton National Forest to discuss our application for a special-use permit, which we would need for the Round River Rendezvous. We met near the trailhead, not far from Brinkerhoff 54, where I worked the night shift. The ranger was very friendly and cooperative, and especially interested in the fact that Ed Abbey would be attending.

While we were standing in the sunshine, the surveyors happened to drive by, recognized the VW van, and pulled into the parking lot. "Arrest these men!" one surveyor demanded.

The ranger was puzzled. He knew Bart and Howie from past encounters and didn't think they were troublemakers. He asked us earnestly if we had been up to the site the day before.

"Yeah, we hiked up to the wellhead," I said.

"Did you see any survey stakes?" asked the ranger.

"Not any that we noticed," I answered.

"Would you like to come down to headquarters and answer a few questions?"

"Not without an attorney," I responded.

We talked to Hank Fibbs. When he was informed of our predicament, he advised, "Don't worry, no jury in Teton County will convict you."

Suddenly we had offers from other attorneys to represent us should we be charged with pulling up the stakes. We were advised not to answer any questions. Meanwhile, the pulling of the survey stakes was receiving statewide media coverage, and was soundly condemned by Governor Ed Herschler, Getty Oil, and the Forest Service. It looked like Teton County, home to movie stars and millionaires, was in open revolt. With all this going on in the background, this year's Round River Rendezvous was going to be very different.

A few days before the 1983 Rendezvous was to begin, I got a call at our official Earth First! headquarters in Moose, Wyoming, a small collection of houses and trailers a few miles east of Jackson. The caller identified himself as Stewart McBride, a freelance reporter working for *Outside* magazine.

Yeah, right, I thought. He wanted to know if there was anyplace he could stay.

"You want a motel?" I asked.

"No, I can't afford a motel," he said. "Can anyone pick me up at the airport?"

Not quite sure what to think, I agreed to pick him up and let him stay in Moose, still not really believing he was from *Outside* magazine. I mean, who would send a reporter all the way to Wyoming without an expense account? People were arriving from all over, and Moose was bustling with activity. McBride was quiet and unassuming, and after a while, we hardly noticed him.

At this time, few people in Jackson had ever heard of Earth First! In an effort to get local people up to Granite Creek to protest at the end of the Rendezvous, I had put up posters announcing that Ed Abbey would be speaking, and left it at that.

It must have succeeded, because on the day of the protest, more than three hundred people arrived, most of them locals. We started off with music by Johnny Sagebrush and the Wild Goose Band, which featured Bob Greenspan on electric guitar and several local musicians. Abbey took a hike up to the well-head and returned with a strip of fluorescent orange tape hanging from his belt. So did many others. The road had once again been completely de-surveyed, in broad daylight, and with the media and the Forest Service present.

Abbey took the stage and delivered a rare speech, short but to the point.

"I see no problem with nuclear power," he said, "twenty million miles away, on the sun. We have a right to be here, but not everywhere, and not all at once." Abbey continued in this vein for a few short minutes and introduced Dave Foreman, who with his "speechifying" got the crowd riled up. By now, the crowd had consumed a considerable amount of beer in the warm sun. Foreman, aping a southern preacher, implored the crowd to get in the road, which they did without delay. Here they were handed every sort of placard voicing their opinion on the proposed road.

Individual letters were assigned to other people spelling out STOP GETTY OIL. Foreman made them all promise to return if Getty ever attempted to build this road. They did. Few of these people had even realized that they were going to a protest when they left the house that morning, but they held their signs and chanted along with Foreman until we all were hoarse, and then we went back to drinking beer around the campfire.

The next day, the protest was featured in the statewide news media, including a front-page photo in the *Casper Star-Tribune,* the state's largest newspaper. Politicians started aligning against the project. Still the Forest Service was going to move ahead and punch the road into Little Granite Creek. Fortunately, the Buckaroos were a pretty bright bunch. Bart found a technicality with regard to Forest Service road right of way over Bureau of Land Management subsurface mineral rights. A small section of the road had not been granted proper approval through the BLM's process.

Bart wrote the appeal on a bar napkin at the Rancher Bar. Howie was there. The Buckaroos were all about business, and business was booming. After the appeal was filed on behalf of the Wyoming Wilderness Association, the governor's office filed a similar appeal. The weight was too much. The Forest Service and Getty Oil buckled. They were both tired of the bad publicity. Little Granite Creek was saved! The Buckaroos had won.

This was good news, but it was not easy to explain to Denny Davis, my driller on Brinkerhoff 54. He had shown up to the protest, as did some of my other crewmates, but the rest of the roughnecks were very angry, and they blamed me for the fact that the rig was going to move somewhere else. A move couldn't possibly be as nice, since Brinkerhoff 54's location in Little Granite Creek was the best location on the best rig in the whole state of Wyoming.

When the tool pusher showed up to give us the news, it was worse than anyone had imagined. Our next hole was at Windy Gap, up Bitter Creek, in the middle of the Red Desert, at 7,500-feet elevation, and a three-hour drive from the closest motels in Rock Springs.

Come October, it was time to move the rig. By now, the snow was setting in and the temperatures were dropping to below zero. Denny made me promise to stay with the crew until the rig was set up at Windy Gap because he was afraid most of his roughnecks were going to "twist off" to see if they could find a better job on a hole that wasn't "too deep, too cheap, and too far to drive."

Setting up Brinkerhoff 54 in Windy Gap would prove to be almost impossible. The trucks were able to unload the sections of the rig, but it was so windy that we couldn't use the cranes to assemble the derrick. When the winds died down, the temperature dropped below zero, making it impossible to unroll the electrical cables to connect the generators to the engines. This could be accomplished only by using a propane torch to heat the cables, while being careful not to melt the rubber insulation. The high winds meant we had to walk backwards and with great difficulty. To make matters worse, a blizzard had set in for a few days and closed all the roads up Bitter Creek with giant wind drifts.

None of that bothered me, because even for the days we couldn't get to the rig, I was still getting a full day's wage. The weather had been so bad that we spent most of the day in an empty truck trailer warmed only by a propane torch. The crew was not happy, but I had promised to stick around until the drill bit was turning to the right, when the heat would be turned on and working conditions would be remarkably better.

When that day at last arrived, I moved back to Jackson. In less than a year, Brinkerhoff 54, Wyoming's newest and biggest rig, fell into disrepair, like a shiny new Cadillac driven by an alcoholic. The difficulty in getting experienced roughnecks to travel out to Bitter Creek proved impossible, and the mighty Brinkerhoff 54 was soon reduced to a pile of junk.

In January 1983, *Outside* magazine ran a feature by Stewart McBride on Earth First! This was to be the first of many articles on the organization, and it set the tone for all the press that would follow. We were now the real Monkey Wrench Gang, outlaw Buckaroos fighting the destruction of the wilderness with bare fists.

In truth, this was a distortion. Besides our bombastic rhetoric, we weren't really that much different from the other conservation groups. Up until that time, we had pulled a few stunts, blocked one road in New Mexico for a day, and staged a few relatively small demonstrations. What made us different was that we were prepared to go on the offensive. Stopping the road legally had deprived us of an opportunity to test our theory that civil disobedience might yet reinvigorate the environmental movement.

Soon, in Oregon, we would get that opportunity. During the next year, Earth First! groups were suddenly springing up everywhere, and that winter I joined the road show as a harmonica player for Johnny Sagebrush along with Foreman, folksinger Cecilia Ostrow, and Australian environmentalist John Seed.

Seed was touring with a movie, *Give Trees a Chance*, about a successful campaign to stop logging in the tropical rain forest of New South Wales. The Australian activists had used nonviolent civil disobedience to block logging and road building, just the sort of things Foreman felt would work here in the United States. We also had our own movie, produced by Hayes, Mc-Cloud, and Switkes, which documented the cracking of the Glen Canyon Dam and featured a rare interview with Ed Abbey.

We traveled nine thousand miles in eight weeks and visited thirty-six cities from New England to Florida, from Portland to Los Angeles, and many stops in between. We did not actually play to packed houses, but there was considerable enthusiasm and several more Earth First! groups were formed in our wake. Foreman was developing his skills as a preacher, and he railed against the Forest Service, whom he called the Freddies, for allowing the corporate takeover of our public lands, which were then slated for destruction. Of particular concern to Earth First! were two new gigantic logging roads, one in northern California and another in southwest Oregon. As we did in Little Granite Creek, we were promising to block the road construction with our bodies.

After leaving Windy Gap, I never went back to the oil patch. Instead, I drove to the Pinacate Desert in Mexico with my roommate Kevin Everhart, a bright guy we affectionately nicknamed Airhead. Airhead also worked for Paul Gilroy as a guide and wrangler. We returned a few weeks later, during a particularly cold spell in Jackson.

When I walked in the door, the house looked as if it had been plundered by a horde of savage berserkers. Clothes covered in mud were strewn about the floor. Part of the floor was ripped up. Spoiled food and dirty dishes were scattered everywhere. The whole place was littered with beer cans and empty bottles of Jack Daniels.

But that was how we had left it, so the mess wasn't the problem. The problem was that someone had left the door ajar, it had blown open, and the pipes had frozen solid and burst. They had frozen all the way down to the bottom of the well and broken the pump. Not only was our house out of water, but so were our upstairs neighbors, two nearby trailers, and another house next door, which was pretty much all of Moose, Wyoming. And it was 30 below outside.

No sooner had I surveyed the damage than the phone rang.

It was Paul Gilroy, the landlord of Moose, Wyoming, whose tenants now had no water. Airhead answered the phone.

"I want you out of my house!" Gilroy bellowed. "What's with all the bullet holes in the kitchen cabinets?"

"They're pellets, Paul, not bullets. We were just shooting at whiskey bottles for target practice and must have missed a few. A man's got a right to keep his pellet gun sighted in."

"And how about that hole in the floor?" Paul asked.

"I can explain that, too," Airhead said.

"Well, don't bother. You boys need to bag your rags and get on down the road," Paul said. "You need to be out by the end of the day, tomorrow."

"That didn't go too well," I observed.

"No, he was pretty hot," Airhead responded. "I think he's serious."

The next day, we had a yard sale in the 20-below weather, and I liquidated all my personal belongings. I had lived in Jackson for over seven years now, and the number of items I'd collected was significant.

I loaded up the *Lumbago*, my 1964 GMC motor home, with what remained and attached my 1972 Datsun 1200 with a tow bar. With that, Airhead and I set out for Oregon. Road construction was slated to knock down critical patches of ancient forest once the snow melted. Oregon had yet to see the face of the new environmental movement. We were determined to make our stand in an area that would be known to all as Bald Mountain.

4

The Rain Forest Icon

Today the rain forests are understood to be important. In school, children learn about their ecological value, and many organizations exist to advocate for the rain forests. In the last twenty years, U.S. groups alone have raised on average over a billion dollars a year to protect them. Laws have been created, reforms promised—and yet we are only minimally closer to saving rain forests than we were fifty years ago, when scientists asserted their importance and decried their imminent destruction.

This assessment will seem harsh to those who contribute to environmental groups working to save the rain forest. Few rain forest groups will admit that their approach has been unsuccessful. Raising larger sums of money has seemed a more important goal than risking a knock-down, drag-out battle with Amazon loggers. This is no accident. The timber industry is a formidable adversary, and it has powerful allies around the world. Like opium growers, timber harvesters will move into new areas when they are pushed out of others. They never give in without a fight.

Conservation groups hate to be written off as extremist. The timber industry exploits that discomfort and uses every tool in their kit to portray conservationists as radicals. The most powerful tool in their arsenal is a vast public relations industry that trains foresters to propagate the religion of forestry and the idea that timber is the principal reason for the existence of these complex forest systems. Using propaganda and pseudoscience, they have fended off criticism of any negative impacts the timber companies have caused. By casting the logger as the central character in a drama that pits conservation of forests against jobs, communities, and the legitimate need for lumber, the timber industry has succeeded in reinventing itself as the underdog. Environmental groups are portrayed as outsiders, self-interested, self-serving, and bureaucratic.

This divisive strategy has worked so well for so long that I can imagine a Roman forester arriving in Lebanon before the first millennium to sweet-talk the locals out of their famous cedars.

Some things never change. The timber industry has operated without regulation or interference for the greater part of its history. The vast majority of laws, rules, and regulations that limit the power of large companies to cut down forests are ignored throughout most of the world. Logging corporations are challenged in their efforts only by citizen conservationist activists and scientists. This group of people working together in the name of the planet comprises the most diverse, broad-based, international social-change movement in history. There is scarcely a city, town, or village on Earth that is not working on some aspect of forest conservation, from the highlands of New Guinea to the Siberian Taiga.

The effort to save the rain forest has been primarily a grassroots movement throughout most of its history. I became involved in 1981, when I started receiving a very curious publication called the *Nimbin News,* printed on an old-fashioned mimeograph machine and rolled up tightly in a scroll. While this format was very difficult to read, it was not long before I awaited each new edition with anticipation. Of particular interest were the writings of a fellow by the name of John Seed, who, as you know, traveled with me and Dave Foreman during the 1982 Earth First! road show. Seed had met poet Gary Snyder in Australia. Snyder had given him some copies of the *Earth First! Journal.* With that, Seed starting sending us the *Nimbin News.*

Seed's story is one that took him from the corporate offices of Sydney to a small community in New South Wales, where he and his friends established Bodhi Farm near the community of Nimbin. Nimbin was home to several new settlers in the region who were fleeing the cities to grow their own food. The idyllic lifestyle was suddenly interrupted in 1979, when a logging company planned to construct a road into Terania Creek, the largest unprotected tropical rain forest in Australia. The ensuing campaign was the first of its kind in a developed country, and it led to the birth of the modern movement to preserve the rain forest.

Seed's involvement in the ultimately successful campaign convinced him that not enough attention was being paid to the rain forest crisis. He started the Rainforest Information Centre and began to organize scientists, politicians, and other opinion leaders to speak out against tropical deforestation not only in New South Wales, but globally as well. The tactics used during the Terania Creek campaign included nonviolent civil disobedience like sitting in front of the log trucks, climbing and sitting in trees, and mild forms of sabotage, including digging up the road and even dismantling a few bulldozers, tactics Earth First! would adopt in Oregon during the Bald Mountain campaign of 1983.

During the 1982 road show, Seed made a significant impression on American environmentalists. Before we set off on the tour, Seed convinced me to do a follow-up to a story I had written about the impact of beef imports from Central America on the rain forests of that region. Since we had identified Burger King as a key importer of rain forest beef, he suggested I organize a campaign to force Burger King to cancel their contracts. I had signed on to the show as a roadie who played harmonica. I would now be giving speeches on the "Hamburger Connection" during each performance. I also passed out a signup sheet to help organize demonstrations at Burger King's restaurants. This simple organizing tool helped me organize seventeen Rainforest Action Groups, or RAGs.

The last performance of the road show was at a Unitarian Church in San Francisco. It featured a reading from Gary Snyder and was attended by a large section of the San Francisco environmental movement, including many crew members of the *Rainbow Warrior*. The *Warrior* was docked close to Fisherman's Wharf in San Francisco. The event was organized by Randy Hayes, the filmmaker from the Glen Canyon Dam "cracking." Randy was a key Bay Area activist and had met John Seed in the San Francisco Friends of the Earth office. Randy had already started a project called People of the Earth to identify and log the names and addresses of all the indigenous environmental groups around the world. To accomplish this, he was using something I had heard of before but never actually seen—a computer.

I was still traveling with a portable Royal typewriter, a ream of carbon paper, and a file box. So was Seed, except he kept his files in a hand-woven bag. There was no time to lose. Seed looked at me, dead in the eye. "Mike, the only thing standing between the loggers and the rain forest are a few people with typewriters. Now you are one of them. Currently there is no grassroots response to the rain forest crisis in the U.S. There is one in Australia and in Europe. But this country is critical for any hope of success. The United States is the place where most of the rain forest's timber and beef are being imported to. U.S. banks are financing these mega-projects like large dams, strip mines, and smelters. It's very important that we launch a campaign. The hamburger campaign will at least be a beginning."

He had me in a corner. I had no choice. Seed continued, "In Holland, Friends of the Earth did a protest with two people in a cow suit, eating trees and shitting Whopper containers. I think we should do that."

"When should we do that?" I asked, afraid of the answer—with good reason.

"Monday!" he declared. And so it was.

Hayes's People of the Earth project was not going well. It was very hard to communicate with folks who lived in such remote conditions. There was a language barrier. There were no phones or faxes in many indigenous offices. The vast cultural divides between those of us who lived in the wealthy northern countries and our neighbors in the tropics had not yet been comprehended. On top of that, Randy's computer kept crashing.

He was ready for a fresh approach. A demonstration was planned, and we went to the pier where the *Rainbow Warrior* was docked to make a cow suit, signs, banners, and other items from scraps of old banners in the ship's hold. Of course, my job was to be the ass end. On Monday, about fifty or so people showed up in front of the Burger King in San Francisco, and the world's smallest environmental group took on the second-largest fast food corporation in the world.

After the demonstration, Hayes had set up a meeting with Herb Chao Gunther, director of the Public Media Center, an environmental media firm.

"We don't do Public Relations," Gunther said. "We are not a PR firm. We do all kinds of media for nonprofit groups, but PR is corporate media."

Gunther proceeded to lay out a plan to build a new group dedicated to protecting the rain forests. I had already formed the Rainforest Action and Information Network, which had about thirty or so local groups, all recruited through Earth First! road shows. The thing about the RAIN name, though, was that there was already a fellow in Portland, Oregon, using that acronym for an alternative-living magazine he published semi-regularly. He was irritated as hell that I was using his initials.

It was at the meeting with Gunther that Hayes and I decided to form the Rainforest Action Network. Gunther committed to helping us raise money, not something you'd expect from a PR firm, but a service that PMC offered its clients, the list of which reads like a who's who of the environmental and social-justice movements.

Recently, Gunther had helped a group called INFACT wage an international boycott against corporate giant Nestlé, a company that was aggressively promoting a powdered baby formula by attempting to convince mothers it was superior to breast-feeding. It wasn't. Nestlé's success in marketing their inferior product was actually increasing incidences of malnourishment in the children who drank it. After six years of pressure, Nestlé relented. Gunther thought we could achieve similar results, but we would have to build our base and raise a lot of money.

Gunther went to work immediately. PMC prepared a press packet and set up a press conference to make a formal announcement. Everything was set. But politics are never predictable— especially when they compete with the forces of nature. An earthquake struck. We were in a bar in the cellar of a skyscraper on Van Ness Avenue. The wineglasses, hung upside down over the bar, began to tinkle. The ground trembled; tables shook. I found it all amusing. But Randy and Gunther didn't, and were now standing in the doorway for protection. I laughed at their reaction, but after a few long seconds of shaking, I realized the quake was serious and joined them in the doorway.

Nothing tops an earthquake story in San Francisco. All interviews, television appearances, and radio talk shows were suddenly canceled. Nevertheless, we got the story out. Demonstrations were spreading to cities and towns across the country, and Burger King was beginning to realize that this problem would not go away.

It would get bigger, in fact. Gunther designed a direct mail piece and began to test it on a few mailing lists purchased from other environmental groups. The mailer was a hit. Money started pouring in, and angry consumers were sending in thousands of postcards demanding that Burger King stop using rain forest beef.

The campaign began in the spring of 1983. It took four years, but by 1987, Burger King was ready to deal. Sales were slumping, by 12 percent in 1987 alone. It was impossible to say whether the boycott was the reason for that sales slump. But it was likewise impossible to say that it had no bearing. There was considerable dissent at Pillsbury, the parent company, which decided to hire new Burger King management.

The new management wanted a clean slate. There were two major problems, in their eyes. First, overexpansion, rising costs, and reduced profits were causing investor panic. That problem was exacerbated by an expensive and monumentally unsuccessful advertising campaign, featuring a nerd named Herb who had never tasted Burger King's signature sandwich, the Whopper.

The second problem was the boycott. Hayes and Gunther had information that the mysterious Burger King Herb would be announced at a Burger King press conference in New York City. Donors were lined up to place a full-page advertisement in the *New York Times* that scooped Burger King and announced that the Rainforest Action Network had found Herb. There was a reason he had not visited a Burger King restaurant: He wouldn't eat rain forest beef.

J. Jeffrey Campbell, the chairman and chief executive of the Burger King Corporation, was the new chairman in charge of Pillsbury's entire restaurant group. The Pillsbury board of directors was meeting in Minneapolis. There was a crowd of protesters outside the conference-room window. Bullhorns echoed down the glass-and-cement canyons formed by downtown skyscrapers. And there was that dang cow again, pooping Whopper containers.

Campbell made the announcement that Burger King would cease importing beef from Costa Rica, where the restaurant chain claimed to be getting only a small percentage of its beef. Campbell, when asked, stated that the boycott had no influence on their decision. He was lying.

This was neither a big story nor a small story. It appeared only in the financial press. Yet in Costa Rica, the decision landed like a ton of bricks on the domestic beef industry. Burger King claimed that it imported only 2 percent rain forest beef. But the cry from the Costa Ricans made the figures seem dubious.

I met Central American agriculture specialist Dr. James Nations over a beer in Austin, Texas. He said Burger King was buying more beef from Costa Rica than it admitted. The problem was that chain of custody was hard to establish. There were no regulations requiring companies that import beef to label the country of origin. "Mike, the beef is boned and frozen in two hundred-pound boxes. Those boxes are shipped to giant warehouses in Miami and become mingled with domestic beef. They are probably guilty, but you will have a hard time proving it."

I decided I needed a second opinion. I met with another prominent biologist, Dr. Daniel Janzen. Janzen told me unflinchingly that if I wanted to save the rain forest, I should eat Costa Rican beef because the country had such well-managed pastures. It was hard to refute Janzen, who had published many books on Costa Rican ecology and was responsible for one of the largest dry tropical forest restoration projects on the planet. In the world of biology, he was a superstar.

I couldn't prove Costa Rica was selling beef to Burger King. I couldn't prove the grazing harmed the rain forest. I had never even been to a rain forest. Janzen was a Ph.D. I was a high school dropout. Something bothered me about Janzen's analysis, though. I had a hunch Nations was right.

I came to realize that Janzen, in order to work in Costa Rica, had to cozy up to the cattle industry. Cows are not a particularly profitable business. But cows are a status symbol no country can go without. Janzen worked in an arid region of

Costa Rica, where cattle caused much less harm. I wasn't sure he actually liked rain forests. Or, maybe he thought there was too much fuss about them.

But the United Nations Environmental Program had listed Costa Rica as having one of the highest deforestation rates in the world, due mainly to logging, burning, and clearing of tropical rain forests to create cattle pasture. Screw Janzen. We went forward with the boycott.

Meanwhile, back in Costa Rica, the government, the cattle industry, the meat packers, and at least one biologist were not very happy. Burger King may have been truthful about using only a small percentage of imported beef. But that small percentage constituted more than 60 percent of Costa Rica's beef exports. Slaughterhouses had to be shut down until new markets could be found.

Costa Rica decided it was time to budge, and contacted us at the Rainforest Action Network. The Costa Ricans said they were willing to concede to our demands—demands I had written on a portable typewriter. They wanted me to go down to Costa Rica for a symposium on the new legislation they had passed to protect rain forests. The law included all the protections we wanted. The stakeholders were meeting to discuss how to implement the new law. All the bigwigs were there, and President Oscar Arias delivered the opening address.

Janzen was there, not happy still. The old bearded professor greeted me with a wary eye. Everyone else was friendly. Alberto, a local rancher and member of the Costa Rican Cattleman's Association, addressed the crowd. "So, here we are," he began earnestly. "We Costa Ricans believed we were doing everything we could to protect our forests. And along came a big

American environmental group to challenge this. Our national pride was hurt, and we fought them. But today, we are here to admit that we can do better. We used to dance the mambo; now we have to learn the lambada."

Afterwards, I met a delegation for dinner at a local restaurant. Janzen declined an invitation, but Minister of Agriculture José María Figueres was there. In 1994, he would become president of Costa Rica. Several other dignitaries attended the meeting as well, including a Burger King vice president. We sat down and were handed menus. A bottle of Scotch appeared on the table. I gazed at the menu and realized I was in a steakhouse. They indicated that I should order first. Was it an honor, or were they testing me? I ordered the biggest steak off the lower right side of the menu.

"Burn it rare," I said in English. Alberto picked up on this and translated my request into Spanish. After a while, the steaks arrived, and a new bottle of Johnny Walker appeared on the table. Cutting into my steak, I noticed everyone watching me with curiosity. Perhaps they thought I was one of those vegetarian animal rights people.

Alberto broke the silence. "Mike . . . How is your steak?"

"Mmm, good, very good," I responded.

"So you say you were the one who researched our industry," he continued. "So that means you were the one that said Costa Rican beef is of low quality. Is that low quality beef, Mike?" He gave me a mockingly stern look.

"No, Alberto. Honestly, this is the best steak I've ever had."

He continued. "You said in your article that all our beef is for export, and that the average Costa Rican eats less beef than the American house cat." He then went on to name all the countries that ate less beef per capita than Costa Rica. It was a long list. "So tell me Mike, what kind of house cat is this, a lion in the zoo? Where did you get this information?"

Now I had the attention of the whole table. I poured another Scotch. "My friends, let me apologize to your country and to you personally. Originally, I obtained that information about the low-quality beef and the Costa Rican diet from an article by Norman Myers, one of the foremost rain forest ecologists. He got the quote from James Nations, an expert on Central American rain forests. I talked to him. He said he got the information from a research paper titled 'Hoofprints on the Forest,' by Douglas Shane. I am still looking for that paper."

It didn't matter. We had won our first campaign. Not only had we reformed the second-largest fast food chain in the world, we also made some good friends in San Jose who really did care about the forest. At the dinner, José María Figueres asked about the boycott. It had not ended. We were still mailing out the direct mail pieces Gunther had designed. José wanted them stopped. I took another bite of steak and told him we would.

Back in San Francisco, Hayes asked me how it went. I informed him on the new laws, the symposium, the excitement of the Costa Ricans, and their request for an end to the Burger King boycott.

"Can't do it, Mike." Randy got real serious. "Countries pass laws whenever they are under international pressure to reform. It looks good on paper, but it rarely translates into real reform. There is no money for enforcement or implementation. Nothing has changed. You drank Scotch with them, and they charmed you. You gave in. We're not suspending the boycott until we see real change in the cattle industry. We can't just declare victory and walk away from the problem. Besides, that mailer is still raising us lots of money."

I thought back to the road that had led us here.

In November of 1985, Randy Hayes convened a major rain forest strategy meeting at Fort Cronkite in Marin County. Activists from India, Africa, Southeast Asia, Canada, and England attended. It was the first global gathering of its sort in the United States, and long overdue. Most of the attendees I knew by name and reputation. Catherine Caulfield, a researcher living in England; Simon Michiru from Kenya; Harrison Ngau Laing from Borneo; Yoichi Kuroda from Tokyo; Brent Blackwelder from the Environmental Policy Institute; Bruce Rich from the Natural Resource Defense Council; and many others made up this fledgling new movement. Hayes also invited a number of Native American activists. John Trudell, Winona LaDuke, and Bill Wahpepah drove in from Los Angeles. Nilak Butler and Coyote, also known as Fred Downey, were there, too.

Hayes's purpose was to learn. "What should we be doing here in the United States to get our boots off the throat of the rain forest?" he asked. "We can't hope for reform in your countries if we don't get reform here. It is our mindless consumption, our desire for cheap imports, and our complete ignorance on the issue that are our biggest problems." For the next three days, we were schooled by this impressive group of conservationists. They suggested that we do three things: pressure the World Bank to stop financing big destructive projects in the rain forest, reduce tropical timber imports into the United States, and end the importation of rain forest beef.

We were well into the Hamburger Campaign. Greenpeace

agreed to take on tropical timber. Friends of the Earth said it would lead the charge on the World Bank. By 1986, we were well on our way to victory with Burger King. Greenpeace had hired someone to work on the timber-import question. Immediately they became embroiled in the social politics that always come along with logging issues. Like deer in the headlights, they froze.

I asked Greenpeace to support a boycott of all tropical hardwoods.

"We need more research, Mike," Campbell Plowden, the new Greenpeace International Tropical Rainforest Director, said. "We're not against logging. We just want to improve the methods."

"Campbell!" I was irritated. "You were one of the best anti-whaling campaigners in Greenpeace. You were the bravest, chaining yourself to the harpoon guns, risking death in a Zodiac to save the whales. What would you say if I suggested that whaling was okay, and that the industry just needs to be managed better?"

"I would say you are crazy! But trees are not whales."

"Campbell, you cannot win a campaign thinking like that. You would never have banned whaling if you thought like that. The timber industry would love nothing better than to enter into a dialogue with you, while they accelerate their assault on the last rain forests. You cannot log a tropical rain forest and expect it to grow back. There is a large body of scientific research that shows this to be true."

Plowden even had the nerve to challenge Hayes and me around the campfire at the 1985 Rainforest Action Network meeting in Fort Cronkite. "You guys better be serious," he said boastfully, "because we are!" Three years later, Greenpeace not only lacked a campaign, but they had no clear policy on the issue either. They were lost in the jungle.

Frustrated, I took some money out of the Earth First! slush fund account and hired two student interns from the University of California at Berkeley and signed on Pamela Wellner, who had a forestry degree and was a former Greenpeace campaigner. The interns, John Green and Tracy Katelman, were in the UC Berkeley Forestry program, one of the best in the world, working under Professor Arnold Schultz, a noted expert on forests. The report came out early the next year, saying that logging rain forests was destructive and unsustainable. The findings were dismissed by pretty much everyone.

In 1986, Hayes went to Malaysia and helped put together the World Rainforest Movement along with Vandana Shiva, John Seed, Martin Khor, and others. In 1989, I traveled to Penang, Malaysia, to attend a meeting of the newly formed World Rainforest Movement, the third such gathering since Hayes's first conference in Fort Cronkite. It was by invitation only, and since Hayes could not make it, he sent me to fill in. Many of the participants in our first RAN meeting were there, along with some of those I hadn't met, including Mohamed Idris, founder of Sahabat Alam, the Malaysian branch of Friends of the Earth. I met Vandana Shiva, representing the Chipko Movement, the Indian grassroots forest network; Marcus Colchester, of Survival International in England; and Harrison Ngau Laing from Borneo. We got down to work immediately. This group included scientists, anthropologists, indigenous leaders from the forest, and religious leaders. By the end of the meeting, we had agreed unanimously on a boycott of tropical hardwoods.

Meanwhile, Catherine Caulfield, author of *In the Rainforest*, the most comprehensive report on deforestation yet written, pressed Friends of the Earth International to oppose a tropical timber boycott due to the negative effects on local economies. Greenpeace followed this position. It was the same position the timber industry held.

It was also wrong.

As Marcus Colchester put it, "Selective logging is exactly that: You select a forest, and you log it. Once timber companies come in with a road, they keep coming back, and even if they don't, and even if they do leave some big trees, others will use the road to log the trees. Once the forests are cleared, the area will become settled by farmers, who will grow subsistence and market crops. The soil is soon exhausted; the farmers go somewhere else, and then the cattle ranchers move in. This is how it always works. Sure, the farmers need land to grow food, but over two hundred million people live in the rain forest with very little farming and even less logging. These people will be displaced, and there simply is no other forest for them to move to. They are being robbed of their land. We have no right to support logging if they don't."

Tropical rain forests contain more species of life than any other terrestrial ecosystem, numbering in the hundreds of millions, with many yet undiscovered.

Environmentalists have always had a problem with forestry by not recognizing it for what it is: dogma. It is too often respected as science and legitimate economic theory, eventually weakening their resolve against deforestation. As always, the loggers were just pawns in the game, moving from boom to bust, from frontier to frontier, following the edge of the world's rapidly vanishing forests, bringing their families, looking for a future somewhere, just wanting to work.

One can like loggers without loving logging. I would rather hang out with loggers than with most environmentalists. They are a tough breed, independent. Like workers everywhere, they have their own culture, their own humor, bred in the dangerous conditions in which they work. Shake a logger's hand, and he will look you in the eye. His eyes, like the eyes of a soldier, have seen things no one but another logger could comprehend. You cannot lecture them about forestry.

The Sierra Club, the World Wildlife Federation, the Audubon Society, Friends of the Earth, even Greenpeace had fallen into a trap. The issue was no longer about whether to log, only where to log. RAN would not fall into this trap. However, we were under great pressure to do so. The World Rainforest Movement called for a boycott, but it also called for sustainable community-based logging. Did such a thing even exist?

Just as in medieval forestry, sustainability was possible. But only if nontimber forest values were put into the equation. What were those values? Hayes and I sat down with a old Mac computer and a six-pack of beer on a sunny afternoon and came up with ten points on sustainability. They ranged from workers' rights, endangered species, pesticide and herbicide use, and most important, protected areas. Large areas must be left undisturbed, even by sustainable logging. Eventually, this document would lead to the creation of the Forest Stewardship Council, an international certifying body composed of all the interested parties, including those living and working in the forests.

The FSC was supposed to get good timber into the pipeline to replace the bad. It does no good to boycott hardwoods if you can't institutionalize a change. Today, the FSC still struggles to fulfill its mission.

Campaigns need iconic targets, and no target is more iconic than Hollywood. Pamela Wellner researched two types of wood, luan and meranti, that constitute the bulk of international imports. Luan and meranti are not species of trees. They are sold under a variety of names, including mahogany. The wood is logged in Indonesia, Malaysia, Thailand, and Borneo—up the Baram River, where Harrison Ngau Laing lived.

Wellner put all the Hollywood studios on notice. Hollywood was up to 2 percent of U.S. luan and meranti exports in its movies and television sets. After one use, the wood was taken to the dump. Wellner had found a substitute product made out of paper and foam that took paint as well as the hardwood panels did. Wellner insisted that the film industry make a commitment to switch. Hollywood refused.

They would be sorry they did.

Wilshire Boulevard is a major artery in Los Angeles. Paramount sits just off Wilshire in the heart of Hollywood. The Paramount Gate, or archway, is one of the most recognizable symbols in town. Normally, you would see chauffeur-driven limousines entering the gate, with actors, producers, directors, writers, all with script revisions, meetings, or lunches to get to. Today was different. At the gate there were seven protesters, each one with their arms inserted in tubes inside fifty-five-gallon drums filled with concrete. The protesters were handcuffed together inside the tubes, which were constructed of hardened steel pipe. The protesters were able to unlock their cuffs with their hands, but the release was inaccessible to law enforcement. The police would later come to call this protest tactic a "sleeping dragon."

There was a back road into Paramount, but this being Hollywood, no one would even think of using it.

"We're important, goddamn it, let us through!"

That wasn't going to happen. Standing in front of the protesters was Wellner and Atossa Soltani, the director of the Los
Angeles RAN office. They were dressed to the nines and talking to a horde of press. There were helicopters in the air. All
traffic was stopped, not by the protesters, but by the cops, who
had cordoned off the whole block.

The press conference was being covered live. Wellner and
Soltani delivered their demands. Lunch for the execs was
blown. But by the dinner hour, Wellner got what she wanted;
an agreement by Paramount to end its use of tropical plywood
and switch to the new panels. One by one, the other studios
followed Paramount. Another American icon, Broadway, also
fell into line. Hollywood always wants to be seen as socially
conscious. The entertainment industry was now an ally. Though
this was an important symbolic victory, it affected only a small
percentage of the global tropical market.

Over the next few years, RAN would continue to win major
concessions from companies that imported timber. Companies
like Home Depot, Mitsubishi, Scott Paper, Canadian timber giant MacMillan-Bloedell, and many others. The strategy was to
pressure the large corporate customers of these timber behe-
moths, firms usually immune to public pressure. Unlike their
suppliers, large retail firms did not have the luxury of ignoring
the wishes of their customers. Pickets at the retail outlets were
always taken seriously, especially when they happened at many
locations over an extended period of time. Additionally, RAN
would invade corporate boardrooms with raucous demonstrations. Other times, they deployed eye-catching direct actions
that included boarding ships from Indonesia loaded with meranti. RAN took out full-page ads in major newspapers, many
designed by Gunther at the Public Media Center. All this activity

threatened to damage the corporate brands, every company's most important asset. The corporations gave in, and we sourced their products in an environmentally sustainable way.

RAN accomplished its goals not only with an aggressive approach, but also by working in coalition with dozens of other groups, large and small. In doing this, they paved the way for other, larger organizations to enter the fray. The rain forest was now an emblematic issue. But like all symbols, it was in danger of having its meaning eroded.

Rain forest conservation has become a large multinational industry with its own interests to get in the way of good policy. The groups involved are not only lost in the jungle, the jungle is lost in the policy. The conservation movement's ongoing failure to aggressively confront the issue of tropical timber imports—long understood to be the principle cause of rain forest destruction—illustrates a substantial weakness insofar as environmental advocacy.

Still, I think there is hope. We must translate the popularity of rain forests into effective on-the-ground measures that protect indigenous people and these precious forests for their true nontimber value.

During the era of the tropical rain forest campaign, I was working dual operations, and became increasingly aware of the illegal destruction of ancient forests occurring right here in my own country.

The most threatened rain forest in the world was in my backyard—the temperate rain forest, which remained on only 0.1 percent of the Earth's land mass.

A battle was brewing in Oregon, as well as in the redwood groves of California. The actions of a few people and the events that followed would change forest history forever.

5

Four Months in a South Dakota Prison—Another Day at the Office

I never should have answered the phone that morning. But I did. It was Greenpeace legend Steve Sawyer. He got right to the point.

"We need you in Rapid City," Steve said. "Can you go?"

Steve is one of the guys at Greenpeace who I could never turn down. It is very difficult to say no to the man who has gone on more missions for the firm than anyone I knew. He had been the skipper of the *Rainbow Warrior* on the day it was bombed in Auckland, New Zealand, by French commandos. The blast killed photographer Fernando Pereira and sank the boat.

"Okay," I said, "I'll go. What do you need me to do?"

"Can't talk on the phone. We'll send someone to pick you up at the airport. Karen Coulter will fill you in."

"When do I need to leave?"

"Tomorrow," he answered.

It was a very short phone call—but one that would change my life for a while. It was October 1987. The next day, Karen picked me up at the airport and filled me in on the scenario. A Greenpeace crew had been in Rapid City for the last week, and most of the preparations for the upcoming action were complete. It turned out that what they really needed most was a mule. That mule was going to be me. I was to carry a one-hundred-pound pack to the top of a mountain in the Black Hills that for centuries had been known as the Six Grandfathers.

The next morning, we arrived at the visitors' center in two rental cars. We got out, unloaded our heavy gear, and headed down a small path that leads to a steel gate. The gate was locked, as expected, so we pulled out a pair of bolt cutters and easily snapped it in two. Climbing up a set of steep metal stairs, we reached the summit of the mountain just after midnight. It was a dark, starry October night, a bit cold, with patches of snow and ice on the ground. We peered down at the visitors' center and its parking lot five hundred feet below. All was still.

I took a deep breath, peeled off my pack, sat down, and muttered, "Sweet Jesus, that was one hell of a hump."

Under my ass was the carved granite forehead of George Washington. From where I sat, I could see the faces of Teddy Roosevelt, Abraham Lincoln, and Thomas Jefferson. We had just climbed Mount Rushmore. It was time to get to work.

I looked over at Bill Keller, who carried an identical hundred-pound pack. My feet hurt from carrying the load on the jagged rubble beneath the steep slope. Inside each of our packs were two halves of a large banner, the largest ever for a Greenpeace protest, at one hundred feet by fifty feet. We began rigging the climbing ropes to the large eye bolts that protruded from the giant heads, and our climbers—Steve Loper, Ken

Hollis, and George Harvey—prepared to go over the edge and down the face of the mammoth sculpture. The goal was to attach a gas mask to the face of George Washington, then suspend the giant banner just below the four heads. The banner read, WE THE PEOPLE SAY NO TO ACID RAIN—GREENPEACE.

The protest was an effort to draw public attention to the problems caused by acid rain, largely a product of coal-fired power plants. A bill was pending in Congress to force power companies to reduce their emissions of sulfur dioxide, the main chemical responsible for acid rain. The bill called for the installation of a new scrubbing technology to remove the corrosive pollutants from the plants' emissions. The industry had been resisting efforts to regulate the power plants, and the fight in Congress was a stalemate between the big industrial states that produced and used the power, and the states directly downwind, which suffered the most severe consequences. A vote was imminent on the new law, and Greenpeace wanted to generate a powerful front-page image that would elevate the debate and help pressure reluctant lawmakers to vote for the controversial bill.

Before the climbers go over the edge, Keller and I say our good-byes to the team and scramble down the back side of the mountain to observe the rest of the deployment from the visitors' center observation deck. I had a handheld radio to keep in touch with the climbers.

From the deck at the visitors' center, everything seemed to be going as planned. The sun was rising, and it was getting warmer. There was no wind. A few early visitors watched in curiosity. The climbers descended to the level of George Washington's nose and attempted to put the gas mask over his chin. A serious problem developed immediately. The mask, designed to go over his face, didn't fit. The designers had not accounted for the fact that the sculpture was a relief. It was an image carved on a surface, like an etching on a coin. But the mask had been designed for a bust, and had the same spatial relationships as a three-dimensional statue. The distance from the nose to the ear was much less on the left side of the face. George was also missing an ear on that side. The makers of the mask had been working from a photograph and had not seen that the appearance of three dimensions was an illusion. Now the climbers were struggling to get the mask on and losing valuable time as the sun rose higher and it became light. It wasn't long before park rangers noticed the guerrilla climbers and quickly began to react.

After what seemed like a long time, the climbers abandoned the gas mask, unable to attach it to Washington's face. They set to work hanging the banner along the steep rock fall below the sculpture. This task required the three climbers to stretch a rope, like a curtain rod, across the slope, and secure it on each end with webbing. Then they attached the banner, pulled it out of the stuff sacks on curtain rings made from carabineers, and pulled it across the slope still rolled up. The trick was to pull it completely taut and then unfurl it by ripping off a few pieces of masking tape wrapped around it. Usually this goes smoothly, and then the climbers descend to the bottom of the banner, securing it, and remaining in place so nobody can cut the banner ropes without risking serious injury to the climbers. On that day, Loper was having trouble. His ropes were getting tangled, preventing him from climbing up to set the knots. More precious time was lost.

Now I could see the park rangers organizing into a small posse. They headed up to the metal gate at the base of the stairway. After climbing a steep trail, they discovered that we had changed the lock on the gate and that their keys didn't work. The tactic had worked. *Good,* I thought, *this will buy us a little more time.* The posse headed back down the hill, leaving behind two rangers to guard the gate. It took the rangers another half hour or more to get down to their vehicles to retrieve a set of bolt cutters. Before long, they were climbing the metal stairs leading to the summit. Soon, I could see their silhouettes on Mount Rushmore's ridgetop.

Flip Templeton, our safety coordinator who had stayed behind to guard the ropes, intercepted the rangers. Flip's job was to make sure that none of the rangers would try to cut the ropes. Flip shouted a warning about the dangers of messing with the lines that held our climbers in the air. The rangers placed him under arrest.

The wind started to pick up. Loper's lines became hopelessly snarled. He began to descend to the ground to try to untangle them. This was considered a risky move employed only as last resort. It's extremely hard to nab a climber on the ropes. But climbers are an easy target on the ground. Loper hit the ground and began to untangle his ropes when a ranger who had been hiding in the brush rushed out and grabbed him, wrestling him to the ground and taking him out of the action.

Ken Hollis would now have to set the knots on Loper's end after he secured his end, which meant a difficult traverse across the steep slope. Before he could get over, though, one of the rangers on the summit started jerking on his line. The ascenders he was using required constant tension on the line. The ranger's actions were putting Hollis in grave danger. Knowing that the rangers already had one of our radios, I barked into the receiver, "Somebody tell that dipshit to quit jerking the rope. He's gonna get someone killed!" Right then, I was seized by two rangers who had been observing the action on the deck.

"You're under arrest for aiding and abetting an illegal act," one of the rangers said as they cuffed me. I was read my Miranda rights and placed in the backseat of the ranger's SUV.

I can't say I was all that surprised. There is always a risk of getting arrested when you're involved in an action. It had happened before. I was more than willing to go to jail with the rest of my team. We weren't expecting any serious reaction from the park rangers. A similar banner supporting a nuclear test ban by Greenpeace on the Statue of Liberty in 1984 had resulted in a small fine by the judge. I sat and watched the rest of the action from the backseat of the police cruiser. Rangers were now rappelling down the side of the mountain on their own ropes to remove our banner. Only half of it was hung, saying proudly, WE SAY NO TO ACID. Fortunately, an Associated Press photographer had taken a photo of this half of the banner with a climber in action, and it was widely distributed, appearing in more than three hundred newspapers in the United States. The caption made no mention of our screwups. Later the acid rain legislation came up for a vote, passed, and was signed into law by Ronald Reagan. We posted bail and agreed to return for court. By evening, I was on my way back home to San Francisco. Just another day at the office—or so I thought.

I returned to Rapid City, South Dakota, to face charges for court in early December of 1987. During our pretrial meeting with the prosecutor, he announced that we would have to serve thirty days and would have to surrender our climbing gear and radios.

"What," we protested, "surrender our gear and radios? You gotta be kidding!"

The radios were issued to our team by legendary Greenpeace radio operator Richard Dillman, who still had the original handheld radio purchased for the first voyage of the *Rainbow Warrior*. Returning to San Francisco without the gear was not an option. We were also surprised by the length of the proposed jail term. While most Earth Firsters could do thirty days standing on their heads, thirty days is a long sentence for a Greenpeacer, even a record. Greenpeacers usually received little or no jail time for their deeds.

And then there was also the issue of a long probation— three years of supervision by a federal prosecutor in Rapid City. I have been on probation most of my life, but all those convictions had been in county courts and could not apply outside the state where the crime was committed. Indeed, I was on unsupervised probation in Oregon when the rangers arrested me. The difference was this was going to be federal probation, which would cover all fifty states. And it would be supervised, meaning I would have to check in regularly with a federal probation officer. If I got into any trouble, even sneaking into a rock concert, I'd go back to jail. This sort of probation would mean I could not be present during any other actions or protests where arrests might be expected. Since such actions are my chief occupation, it would effectively put me out of business.

Our team talked briefly with attorney Bruce Ellison and opted to go to trial. Maybe we could get a better deal if we made our case to a jury. This being Greenpeace, I let the lawyers handle everything. That was a mistake. When I got to the courthouse and met with my codefendants and Ellison, I was informed that we were not going to trial, but would have a hearing where we would stipulate the facts to the judge and explain our reasons for breaking the law and putting ourselves at his mercy. The judge in this case proved to be without mercy. A month earlier, he had sentenced a homeless man to twenty years in prison for eating a slice of pizza he had taken out of a convenience store oven when the clerk wasn't looking. In South Dakota, entering a business with the intention of stealing even a slice of pizza is considered felony burglary. I agreed to go along with the legal strategy, although on its face, things did not look good.

Our plan was that in addition to stipulating that we had committed the offense for a greater good, the lawyers wanted us to take the stand and try to demonstrate to the judge that we were all upright, wholesome American citizens unworthy of a long jail sentence. That was a good idea for most of my codefendants, whose only prior arrests had been for political protests, and mostly while working for Greenpeace. I, on the other hand, had a criminal history going back to my early childhood. A lot of it had nothing to do with politics. One cop described my rap sheet as a "phone book." This was not going to be pretty.

The judge promptly found us guilty. We all received sentences of four months in federal detention with three years of supervised probation. He would suspend three months of the sentence until the successful completion of the probation, which meant that we would have the remaining three months of our sentence hanging over our heads for three years, and any violation of any law could send us back to jail. We were given the option of returning later to report to the county jail in Rapid City, but we had come prepared and decided to go straight to jail.

Once we were in the jail, we were offered a chance to do community service and stay at the work-release center, which they informed us was much better than being in the county lockup. We were told we'd be able to get out into the community performing public service, which proved untrue. Ken Hollis and George Harvey were vegans. They ate no meat, eggs, or cheese. The sheriff told them the only way they were going to get enough fresh vegetables to eat was to volunteer to work in the kitchen, and they promptly did so. For the next thirty days, they would be woken at 4 A.M. to prepare and serve breakfast, followed by a short break and then lunch, another short break and then dinner and cleanup. By the time they had finished one shift, it was 8 P.M. and they had to get some sleep to be ready to start over at 4 A.M. with no days off. Loper was put on some construction job for the county, Flip was cleaning out police cruisers, and I was sent out to sweep up after a Knights of Columbus bingo game at a local community center. Still, it could have been worse, and we resolved to cool our heels for a month.

The work-release center turned out to be a huge windowless dormitory made up of what looked like cheap double-wide mobile homes. It housed forty inmates who slept in four rows of old army surplus bunk beds. It had a large dayroom with tables and chairs. The doors and walls were so flimsy that the whole building shook when anyone walked across the floor. Showers were taken in a large open room. I woke, ate, and slept according to a preset schedule. When I wasn't working, I was allowed only to sit in the dayroom, which was furnished with tables and benches and one small television on a high shelf. It was usually tuned to professional wrestling or, even more popular, the television show *Cops*.

At first I thought this would be some easy time. The food was bland and starchy. The air was bad from too many cigarettes, but it was clean and quiet, and everyone was friendly. The first thing I noticed in a South Dakota jail was the large percentage of Lakota inmates. Most were federal prisoners, like me, from the Pine Ridge and Rosebud reservations just to the north of us. And like the non-Indian population in the work-release center, many were in for minor alcohol-related crimes. Being an environmentalist, I was pretty well shunned by the non-Indian population. Most of the prisoners had seen the television coverage. Hell, we were rated one of the top-ten news stories of the year by the local newspaper. I think they felt like we were showboats, a bunch of privileged kids who had the luxury to protest and were getting paid for it. The Indians, on the other hand, had no problem with our politics, and before long I was more comfortable playing cards on their end of the dayroom. Although I would always have to go back during mealtime and eat with the white guys.

In any jail, the hardest part is the boredom. You can only read or write so much, watch so much professional wrestling, and sooner or later you wind up with absolutely nothing to do. I tried to establish daily routines for reading, writing, and exercising. It doesn't help alleviate the boredom, but it does make the time pass faster. I began to regret doing my sentence in the work-release center. This was much worse than any county jail I had ever been in. I had to find a way out.

I wasn't thinking of breaking out, although that would have been easy enough. Escapes were of no great concern here. The door was never locked on the inside. If you left without permission, you needed to be let back in by a guard who sat at a desk in the dayroom. There was a guard at this desk every day, around the clock. He had a set of small, grainy, black-and-white television screens in front of him. From the command post, he monitored the half-dozen video cameras set in strategic locations around the prison.

He could observe your actions, no matter where you were, even in the bathrooms and showers. That was the worst part. The guards were in your cell 24/7, making regular rounds, walking past your bunk even when you slept—the hard soles of their shoes against the floors sending echoes through the night. In a jail, the guards are not in the cell with you, and they leave you alone at night. This was more like a juvenile detention center. We were not being treated like criminals, but rather like children. Our every action was being monitored, and there were so many rules that by day four I had racked up a score of demerits. Eventually they were going to kick me out of this place. I just needed a few more, I thought, and I'd be lying around in general lockup, playing Monopoly and watching television with no one to tell me what to do.

On day seven of my time in the work-release center, I left on a furlough to go to an Earth First! meeting in Boulder, Colorado. I had told the judge at the time of my sentencing I was supposed to attend a conference, and had already purchased an airline ticket. He gave me permission and told the jailer to add the time I was gone to the end of my sentence. The Earth First! meeting was three days long. During my leave, I got to see my fiancée, Karen Pickett. We had to postpone our wedding when I called and told her I wouldn't be coming home for a while. She was used to me going to jail, but this sentence had taken both of us by surprise. In many ways, I was more afraid of marriage than I was of jail, so I was getting along. Like all Earth First! meetings in those early days, it was also a three-day party. After a week in detention, it was good to be amongst so many friends.

Afterwards, I boarded a plane in Denver and flew back to Rapid City to check back into the work-release center. The next morning, when the roll call came, we were all supposed to line up in rows and wait for our assignments. Jerry supervised the center. He had greasy black hair and a pencil-thin mustache. Every morning, he would read out the work assignments and ask for volunteers. If there were no volunteers, he would just give someone the assignment. I never volunteered. Others did to make sure they didn't end up with a dirty assignment. My last assignment involved being marched in chains through the streets of Rapid City in my hot-orange jail jumpsuit. I was escorted by two armed cops to the Knights of Columbus lodge to mop up after the nightly bingo game. I made the march holding a paper bag with a bologna sandwich in it.

This morning I was in no mood to mop up the bingo parlor, or to be frog-marched through downtown Rapid City in sub-zero weather. Besides, I had been reading the federal regulations and found that I could not be forced to work outside the jail facility. Usually, when you do work release, you get your time cut in half. Every day you work, you go home a day earlier. But I did not qualify for "good time." Unlike the cases of other prisoners, the judge had specifically ordered that the Mount Rushmore protesters not get any time off for good behavior. I wouldn't be let out a day earlier, or even one minute sooner. I was supposed to get out at midnight. So why behave?

When Jerry called out the assignments and got to the Knights of Columbus job, I stood in line and said nothing. He looked hard at me, and I looked back at him, trying to display no emotion.

"Roselle." He called my name again. I stood and remained silent, still looking at him. "Roselle, you got to go to the Knights of Columbus."

"I ain't going," I said.

"Are you refusing an assignment?" he asked me.

"I ain't working for the pope," I said.

At this point, Jerry got upset and warned me that if I didn't volunteer, he would put me in lockdown. Again, he ordered me to go back to the bingo parlor. I was prepared for this, so I tried to argue the law. "As a federal prisoner," I said, "I cannot be compelled to do work outside the jail unless it is on federal property, and certainly I cannot be forced to work for a religious organization," I explained.

"Are you refusing the assignment?" he asked again. It was now very quiet in the room.

"That's correct," I replied. "I'm not working for the pope anymore!"

The room grew less silent, and eventually the other prisoners started snickering. Jerry ordered me to go to my bunk. I went and waited until roll call was over. Normally you are not allowed to be in your bunk until lights-out at ten o'clock. I read my book for a while, and then got bored and decided to go out in the dayroom to get a cup of coffee. I sat and talked with the other inmates who were too old or too sick to work much and watched the news on television. Seeing I was in the dayroom, Jerry again ordered me to my bunk.

"I ain't going back to my bunk, Jerry! I'm just going to sit here and drink my coffee!" I yelled at him. By the time the words left my mouth, I knew I was gone from there. Jerry got on the radio and said they had a situation in the work-release center. Almost immediately, a group of four fully armored men with batons and wearing riot helmets came through the door. The scene was still. They looked at Jerry.

"What's the problem?" one of them asked.

"Roselle won't go to his bunk," Jerry replied.

The big cop looked at me. "Is this true?"

"Yes," I said respectfully.

Offering no resistance, I was cuffed, chained, and marched across the parking lot to the jailhouse. I was going to the county lockup, I thought, where I envisioned that I would be allowed to sit around in a real cell with a bunch of real convicts, watching television whenever I wanted and playing Monopoly.

I was quickly placed in an eight-by-eight-by-eight cement windowless room on the high-security block, which had only twenty-four cells. It contained some of the prison's most violent offenders and a few drug dealers. We were allowed out of our cells only once a day for an hour. We could use the dayroom, where we could exercise, make a five-minute phone call, or play pool. All those things required a wait in line with up to twenty-three other high-security inmates. So usually I stayed in my cell unless I needed to make my five-minute phone call. A five-minute phone call usually took up the whole hour, though, because I was always last in line. Waist chains and leg irons were placed on us before we could leave the cell, so shooting pool was a bit tricky. And the other inmates wouldn't let me go near the lone weight-lifting machine. Otherwise, I was treated with respect, even though I was the only one on the block in there for a misdemeanor charge.

"They put you in here for hiking off trail without a permit?" they would ask with disbelief. "What the fuck is that all about?"

This had gone on for about a week, when Jerry came into my cell. "What do you want?" I asked him before he could say anything. After all, this was my cell, not his work-release center.

"I want to know if you're ready to report back to the work-release center."

"Fuck no," I said. "I like it better here. Get the fuck out of my cell." He left but would come back every week or so to see if I had changed my mind. He always got the same response.

I stayed in solitary confinement for three weeks until my thirty days were up. From solitary, I had had no contact with my codefendants back in the work-release center, except for occasional notes wrapped in aluminum foil and buried in my mashed potatoes. Since my cell number was written on my covered tray, Hollis and Harvey would load it up with extra goodies, usually cake or cookies, which went undetected to my cell.

Finally the day came to appear for our probation hearing. When they took me to the courthouse, I spotted Loper, Hollis, Templeton, and Harvey as they hustled me down the hallway.

"We've all signed the probation papers. Are you going to sign?" Loper asked loudly as he was being taken back to his cell.

"Probably not," I replied. This was something we had all discussed, and I knew that the rest of the team wanted to get out of jail and get back to work. I could respect their decision, but something bothered me about the situation, and that something was the judge. I was unwilling to grovel at his feet, and dreaded the thought of being under his supervision for three years. But there was the issue of doing ninety more days in that eight-by-eight cell. I still had not made up my mind.

I said good-bye to the other Greenpeacers, who were all heading through the steel door that led outside to the sunshine, something I had not seen for more than three weeks. The guards walked me farther down the hall and put me in a small room with a table and two metal chairs and told me to wait.

When the probation officer arrived, he was a tall, thin, grim man wearing a dark suit and holding a manila file. Without exchanging any pleasantries, he introduced himself and began to outline the requirements of my release. "First, you have to hold down a regular job," he said.

"What is a regular job? I am an Earth Firster. Is that a regular job?" I was serious.

"Who pays you?"

"Nobody. I raise money selling bumper stickers and T-shirts." I was still being serious.

"Well," he said, "you'll have to provide us with your tax returns to prove this."

"I thought you guys already had that info."

"You'll have to fill out these forms."

"Okay, what else?"

"You'll have to keep regular hours."

"All right, what are regular hours? Do you meant to say that I can't sleep in and work late? Do I get to stay out late on Saturday night? What are regular hours?"

The probation officer gave me a stern look, as if to say that this is no time for joking. Only I wasn't.

"Put those papers back in the file. I'm not signing them," I calmly told him.

"But, but if you don't sign—," he stammered.

I cut him off. "I know what is going to happen. I'd rather be in my cell doing my time than sitting in here with you. Can I go now?"

The probation officer stood up, opened the door, and the guard let him out of the room, leaving me there. After a while I was taken back to the jail lobby, and I changed into my jail uniform—the orange jumpsuit. I hadn't worn my street clothes since I'd been let out for the Earth First! meeting. On the way back to check into the jail, I had smoked a joint, which I couldn't finish, so I stuck it in my sock. I was wearing two pairs of athletic socks and had put the remains of the joint in between them. When I took the sock off, as required, nothing came out and nothing was visible inside. I put the socks back on, and they took me to my cell.

Now, here's where things got weird. I went back to my cell and waited until after dinner before smoking the joint. I got a toilet paper roll and took the cardboard tube out of it, cut a small X on one end, and pushed my finger through to make a small round hole. I added a piece of aluminum foil that was used to send me contraband food messages from the kitchen, and now I had a pipe. I broke the joint up and took a small piece, saving the rest for later. I took one hit and held it deep in my lungs for as long as I could. When I exhaled, all hell broke loose.

The marijuana had been grown by a close friend in southern Oregon, and it had a particularly strong aroma, which by now had permeated the entire twenty-four-cell block of the high-security, but badly ventilated, wing of the jail.

An inmate began yelling out, "I smell weed! I smell some really *good* weed! Who's got the weed?"

The other inmates soon chimed in, and the whole cell block started going crazy. Not knowing exactly how to deal with this situation, I started yelling out my small window, too, as loud as any of them. But the guards had not smelled it, I thought, and did not know what the fuss was all about. After a few minutes, the cell block calmed down. I took out a miniature AM/FM radio that I had been allowed to keep by one of the nicer guards, even though it was forbidden. She said I could play it as long as I used the earpiece and kept it out of sight. When the other guards shook down my cell, I stuck it under the stainless steel toilet in my cell with some contraband chewing gum I kept for that purpose. I lay back on my bunk and listened to the local college radio play hits from the '60s. I was trying to prepare myself for the next ninety days I would spend in this cell. I wondered if one of these days I might just take Jerry up on his offer to go back to the work-release center. The thought gave me the shivers.

I was still listening to my earpiece when two federal marshals busted in my cell right before midnight.

"What's up?" I asked them, a little startled at seeing two feds in dark suits standing over me.

"You're under arrest," one of them said. "No shit," I replied. "I'm in jail, for chrissakes!"

I was hoping this was not about the joint I had smoked earlier. It seemed unlikely, so I asked them, "What am I under arrest for?"

"Violating your parole," the fed said.

"That's funny, I haven't been out of my cell for three weeks, and my sentence isn't even up until midnight." I still wasn't sure if this wasn't about the marijuana. But they were right: By not signing my probation agreement, I had violated probation. I was read my rights and taken downstairs in cuffs and leg irons, fingerprinted, had mug shots taken again, and then I was deposited back in my cell about an hour later, minus the radio and earpiece.

I settled back in my bunk and tried to figure my situation out, but it didn't make any sense to me. Only later did Bruce Ellison inform me that the judge and prosecutor were taken by surprise when I refused to sign the probation agreement. Under the law, I would have had to be freed by midnight at the latest. They knew I had a plane ticket back to California, and that they would have to arrest me there and send me back for my hearing. Since I was a federal prisoner, I had to be arrested by a federal marshal whose office was in Fargo, two hundred miles away. The feds had driven as quickly as they could to get to Rapid City by midnight. The judge was livid, and he told Ellison that if he'd known I wasn't accepting probation, he would have given me the maximum six months instead of four. But there was nothing they could do except schedule another probation hearing with the judge the next morning. The whole hearing took less than three minutes, and I was sentenced to ninety more days in the hole. The judge scowled at me and left the courtroom. Again I was taken back to my cell.

Now I had to take stock of my decision. If this was going to be home for the next three months, I would need something to do. Since I was trained to be a campaigner, I decided to launch a campaign. The food in that South Dakota joint was something nasty and unhealthy. Most of it was sodium-rich government-surplus canned food and noodles. Rarely were there any fresh vegetables. The feds were paying the county jail for my upkeep, but the county simply didn't want to spend that money on me. So from that day on, I wrote a letter a day to someone in the jail administration to ask for fresh fruits and vegetables. I received no response from anyone.

So I drafted a petition and used my hour in the dayroom to get signatures. No one was interested in signing it. They thought the food was okay, but they were upset that they were no longer able to get salt or pepper. The condiments had been removed from the menu ever since one shackled convict threw pepper in a guard's face and attempted to run across the parking lot in a pathetic attempt at escape. He didn't get very far. But the salt and pepper were missed. The issue was an important one, and heartfelt amongst the constituency. I quickly added a request for salt and pepper to the end of the petition. It was signed by everyone. We received a prompt response. I was taken from my cell for a meeting with the jail staff, including the sheriff and Jerry. They introduced a woman they said was a licensed nutritionist. She explained how the jail menu was perfectly healthy.

"I want to see her license," I demanded. The room became quiet. The sheriff ended the meeting. Again, I was taken back to isolation.

The next morning, I asked to see the nurse. My complaint was constipation. My real problem was the combined effects of no sunlight, little or no exercise, and the steady diet of salt, starch, and canned government beef. They were taking a toll on my body. I felt pasty and sluggish. I pleaded my case to the nurse. She was sympathetic. Not only that, but she said she had raised the issue with the sheriff before, telling him she thought the food was really unhealthy.

"Filing a health complaint really helps back me up on this," she told me in confidence as I left.

The next morning in the dayroom, I told all the guys that they should be asking to see the nurse and complaining about their health. By this time, they were getting a little more interested in the campaign, and maybe, just maybe, they would soon be able to put salt and pepper on their food again. The day after that, two marshals arrived at my cell and told me to grab my property. They shackled my feet, cuffed my hands behind my back, and put me into a large SUV. They were driving me away from Rapid City. They gave me no explanation why, but when I arrived at the Pennington County Jail in Pierre, South Dakota, the jailer there was even more curious than I was.

"Why are they sending you here from Rapid City? We usually send our prisoners over there. You must be some bad hombre."

"Not really," I replied. "I'm a model prisoner. You won't get no trouble from me!"

I was later to learn that they were pretty fed up with me in Rapid City. Not just the daily harassment over the menu, but the fact that I still refused to go back to the work-release center, where one cop could guard me and thirty-nine other prisoners, feed us slop, and keep me in the high-security wing. They had gambled that I would break under the pressure. When I didn't, it caused a problem. Due to overcrowding, it made little sense to keep a nonviolent offender in maximum security. They were just trying to teach me a lesson. They wouldn't put me in the general population in Rapid City. If they did, the other inmates would see it was possible to get placed in a proper jail. That's the reason they place you in solitary confinement in the first place. So you'll go back to the work-release center and do what you are told.

And so it was that after forty days on the maximum-security block with South Dakota's most hardened criminals, I was finally going to be able play Monopoly and serve the rest of my four-month sentence in a real jail. In Pennington County Jail, I had no problems with the jail staff, and since they sent their long-timers to Rapid City, I was the only one there, which gave me seniority, a very important thing in jail. One of the guards was even a member of Greenpeace. They put a phone in my cell and allowed me to talk all I wanted as long as the calls were collect. People could even call me. In this way, I was able to continue working on organizing Earth First! actions, even sending out thousands of fund-raising letters from my cell in envelopes the jail provided. On April 15, at exactly midnight, I was allowed to put on my street clothes and was released from the Pennington County Jail.

I readied to walk from the jail, when the jailer stopped me. "First you'll have to sign these release forms."

"Like hell I do," I barked at him. "I've done my time."

With that, I walked out of the jail and into the lights of the news cameras to talk with the local press.

6

Why I Quit Spiking Trees

The stillness of the evening was broken only by the sound of pounding, as hammers drove large metal spikes deep into the bark of ancient trees. The giant Doug firs up Pyramid Creek in Oregon were 1,600 years old and slated for destruction. The year was 1985.

"Let's mark this timber sale and go!" I yelled to George, a door-to-door environmental canvasser. Karen pulled spray paint and plastic tape out of her pack. Norman, a freelance writer, kept banging away.

My hands hurt. A mean-looking blister had formed on my thumb with each swing of the hammer. All in all, we would be putting twenty pounds of spikes into one hundred trees. Each tree would be marked by a fluorescent-orange ribbon and spray-painted with a large S, for "spiked."

Twenty pounds of spikes is enough to stop the loggers for only a few days. More important, it would send a message to the U.S. Forest Service that we would now be going on the offensive to stop logging in these last remaining stands of oldgrowth forest.

I had spiked trees before and made little secret of it.

In the fall of 1984, the Forest Service announced at a joint press conference with the local Sierra Club that they were going to allow old-growth forests to be logged on Hardesty Mountain, a popular hiking area near Eugene, Oregon. Afterwards, I told the media that just because the Sierra Club gave in didn't mean the fight was over.

I went over to where Forest Supervisor Michael Kerrick was sitting with Waldo Lake Wilderness Committee's Doug Norlen, Oregon Natural Resource Coalition's Andy Kerr, and some other high-level Forest Service staffers in the back of the hearing room.

Within hearing range of Kerrick, I said to Norlen, "Doug, I'm going up to Hardesty Mountain, but first I'm going to the hardware store to buy a box of spikes." Then I glared at Kerrick. A few weeks later, spikes were found in the old trees slated for logging on Hardesty Mountain.

I was questioned by the media, but not by federal law enforcement agents. They seemed to want the whole thing kept quiet, lest it encourage copycat spiking. That could get real messy. While not admitting any involvement, I nonetheless refused to condemn the tree spikers, insisting that it was the U.S. Forest Service breaking the law.

I was mad. Nobody seemed to want to do anything to stand up to the loggers. Environmentalists were satisfied to hold a press conference where one reporter showed up. They felt lucky if a small story appeared in the back of the paper.

Maybe it was Russell Lande's press conference that put me

over the edge. It featured the population biologist's latest findings. His report confirmed what enviros had been screaming
about for years: too much logging had already occurred on the
National Forest, resulting in the decline of a bird called the
northern spotted owl. "What are you going to do about it?"
asked one reporter from *The Oregonian*. The stuffed-shirt environmentalists at the table just shuffled their feet and looked at
each other. It was a sad moment.

The only avenue they could conceive of was to sue the bastards. Everyone knew that wasn't going to happen. The big
dogs in Washington, D.C., and San Francisco had long ago
decided that one does not use the Endangered Species Act to
shut down logging. They thought the public backlash would
result in Congress weakening or even overturning the Endangered Species Act.

But what good is the Endangered Species Act if you don't
use it to protect the most endangered ecosystem on Earth—
temperate rain forests? And there was not just one owl, but
thousands of species of plants and animals at stake.

Yet no one wanted to take on the timber industry. It was
better if you just tried to get along with them.

The industry was too entrenched, both politically and cul-
turally, in the communities where they operated. The timber
beasts pumped a lot of money into the economy, even if that
money came from liquidating one of the greatest forests that
ever grew on planet Earth. And, of course, they owned the politicians.

There may have been hippies in the Oregon countryside
and artists in Portland, but in 1985, Oregon was still dominated by Big Timber. Recreation and technology jobs were
knocking on the door. We were witnessing the equivalent of

the last buffalo hunt. When these trees were cut, the industry was going to shut down. As they had in the Northwoods of the Midwest, the Big Thicket of eastern Texas, and everywhere else the big trees have been eliminated.

I did not think spiking the trees on Hardesty Mountain would prevent them from being logged. But I did think that by making a big stink over it, they might think twice before coming back to cut again.

Sure enough, it did raise a stink.

Eventually, the Forest Service would send a couple dozen forest rangers up the mountain with metal detectors to find and pull the spikes. Then they cut down the giant, moss-covered trees, loaded them onto trucks, and hauled them away. The television cameras came and recorded it all for the evening news.

The next year, 1985, Pyramid Creek was where we drew the line. We tried an appeal. We wanted to sue, but couldn't. Groups with more money didn't want to insult the Forest Supervisor, who, after all, was in charge of planning more clearcuts.

One did not want to piss *him* off.

Actually, I wanted to piss him off. And this time, I wanted the world to know that I spiked this timber sale because I thought it was illegal. Come and get me, Freddies! Let's have a dialogue about these trees and what your buddies in Big Timber are doing on the public lands.

The timber sale covered a little over eleven acres. The trees were huge, some of the oldest in Oregon. We had named this area the Cathedral Forest. With the low light of the evening sending god beams through the canopy high overhead, it felt like we were in some medieval gothic church.

We hammered away until dark, packed up our tools, and drove back into town. In October, we sent out a press release, announcing that the trees were spiked. As with Hardesty Mountain, the local news media was all over the story. I did several interviews and stated that Earth First! had spiked the trees, and that I spoke for Earth First! When asked if I had personally spiked the trees, I repeated that Earth First! had spiked the trees, so yes, as an Earth Firster, I do take responsibility. To prosecute me, they would need another witness. There weren't any.

Tree spiking certainly was an escalation in tactics. Since the days of John Muir, in the late nineteenth century, conservationists have been trying to protect the ancient forests, and without much success. Conservationists have always been derided as tree huggers, druids, hippie backpackers, wealthy elites, or just city people who didn't understand the country.

Timber companies mounted aggressive countercampaigns to squash any effort to save the old growth. Loggers would threaten and intimidate anyone who spoke out against this wasteful practice, and it took a pretty brave person to stand up for the forests in these rural regions. The big-green environmental organizations had all but given up the fight, and the local environmental groups had grown too used to losing.

Once while I was taking a walk with poet Gary Snyder, he recounted to me his thoughts about the Cascades on a hike he took just after the United States had dropped atomic bombs on Japan. "I thought that cities like Hiroshima and Nagasaki would rise and fall, and these mountains would be here forever," he said. "But now, both Hiroshima and Nagasaki are large bustling cities again, and these mountains have all but been destroyed by the timber industry in the years since the war ended."

I was new to Oregon politics, having spent the last eight years in Wyoming. I was with Dave Foreman and Bart Koehler, fellow Earth Firsters. We were, frankly, tired of getting our asses kicked. True, we would win a battle here and there, but when it came to old-growth forests, we were losing the war.

We decided it was time to take a page out of the civil rights playbook and use nonviolent civil disobedience to obstruct the logging. This was our game plan for the upcoming logging on Bald Mountain, in the middle of the Kalmiopsis Wilderness in the Siskiyou Mountains. The Bald Mountain Road was a controversial project costing millions of dollars for a paved logging road into the heart of the roadless area.

Our next stop was the U.S. Forest Service Regional Headquarters in Grants Pass, where we introduced ourselves to District Ranger Bill Butler. Bart, Dave, and I were wearing our cowboy hats and boots, just like back in Wyoming.

He asked who we were.

"Earth First!" we replied.

He had never heard of us.

"We are going to stop the Bald Mountain Road," Koehler told him, almost nose to nose. Butler seemed a bit surprised, even shocked, that anyone would barge into his office and threaten to stop his prized project. Ranger Butler thought this fight, which had gone on for over a decade, was finally over. Who were these cowboys from Wyoming telling him they were going to stop his road?

"What are you going to do?" Butler asked. The fact was, we really didn't know. We had never attempted anything like this before. As far as we knew, no one else had either.

"We'll be in touch," I said, giving him my new Earth First! business card. My name, Mike Roselle, appeared under the title

Outside Agitator. As we walked down the stairs and were getting ready to leave the building, we were approached by a Forest Service employee who was standing by the door. He looked
around cautiously and asked where we were going.

"To the bar," said Bart. "Do you know a good dive around
here that serves cheeseburgers?"

"The Wonder Bur, downtown," he said. In a low voice he
continued, "Look, I can't talk here. But I'd like to meet you at
the bar later. If they see us talking, I could get transferred out
of this office and sent to Forest Service Siberia."

Later, he entered the bar. It was a logger bar, and they
didn't like the Freddies any more than we did, but for opposite
reasons. "I'm Mike Amaranthus, and I am a biologist for the
Forest Service," he offered. "I was on the team that prepared
the Environmental Impact Statement for the Bald Mountain."

"You oughtta be proud," Koehler grumbled as he ate his
burger and washed it down with Budweiser. "How can anyone
claim that a paved two-lane, logging road in the middle of a
wilderness area has 'no significant impact'?"

"Good question," said Amaranthus. He went on to describe
how he became suspicious when District Ranger Butler asked
for the scientific team's original notes. When the Final Environmental Impact Statement was released, it omitted the team's
findings. Amaranthus asked to see the report he submitted, as
well as those of the other biologists. Ranger Butler said the
paperwork was in Portland. Amaranthus went to Portland,
where he was told the notes were sent to headquarters in
Washington, D.C. Since he had to attend a meeting at the HQ
anyway, he took the opportunity to ask to see the notes and
files. There were no files. They had vanished into thin air.

"So don't blame me," Amaranthus said. "I'm one of the few

people to have actually seen this place. It's like no place on Earth. None of us thought it should ever be logged. Not only is this some of the best old-growth forest habitat in the state, but the slopes are too steep and the soils too unstable to prevent massive erosion from taking place. The silt will wipe out the salmon runs by burying their spawning beds."

It was unbelievable, but not entirely shocking to us.

"What are you guys going to do?" he asked.

"Somehow, we're going to stop it!" was my reply.

Before leaving, Mike gave us his card and wished us luck.

Now we had a mission: Save Bald Mountain! So we began to organize around the state. Down in the mill town of Grants Pass, at a meeting of local environmentalists, civil disobedience was a tough sell. Sure, the local activists had thought about doing this before. Many locals were veterans of the civil rights or antiwar movements. Some had been arrested protesting nuclear power. They had even occupied clear-cuts to prevent the spraying of toxic pesticides in their watersheds. But most thought civil disobedience in the woods was too risky. You were a long way from the nearest police station, and if violence broke out, you would be on your own.

In the end, only two Oregonians and two guys from Wyoming were willing to risk staging a blockade. The bulldozers were already sitting at the gravel pit on Flat Top, waiting for the snow to melt enough to cut a road out of the mountainside and over into Silver Creek, centered in the largest old-growth forest on the West Coast.

Coming in from Briggs Creek, on the banks of the Illinois River, we hiked fourteen miles through the night. The road crew had already started work on the approach, and was sending a D-9 Caterpillar toward the ridge leading into the headwaters of Silver Creek, on Bald Mountain's north side. At that moment, Steve Marsden, Pedro Tama, Kevin Everhart, and I dropped down onto the road and linked arms in the path of the oncoming bulldozer.

Driving the bulldozer was Les Moore, the crew boss from Plumly Construction Company, which had the contract to build the road. We had introduced ourselves to Les and his crew the week before, when they were eating lunch by their trucks, listening to Paul Harvey's talk radio show.

Shaking Les's hand, I had looked him in the eye and said, "When you guys start, we are going to be here. We just want you to know. We are not going to damage your equipment or be violent in any way, but we are going to stop this road."

Now Les was roaring full throttle toward the end of the grade where we were standing. But if he thought we were going to get out of the way, he was soon disappointed. Seeing that we wouldn't play chicken, he stopped the dozer and lowered the blade.

"What the hell are you idiots doing?"

He got off the dozer and walked back and forth in front of us, yelling insults like a drill sergeant, threatening to get his boys to come over and take care of us.

We remained calm. He got back on the dozer, backed up, lowered the blade, and scraped up a four-foot-high pile of dirt and gravel, pushing it toward us, until it started to cover our feet and halfway up the calves of our legs. We didn't move. When that didn't work, Les backed up the dozer again, lowered the blade, and turned off the engine. He rose out of his seat, dismounted the cab, took off his hard hat, threw it on the ground, and went walking back the quarter mile to the staging area where we had met just the week before.

The news media had been alerted that something was going to happen and were promptly led to the end of the road by Dave Foreman. We all did interviews. Then the Josephine County sheriff showed up and hauled us to jail, three and a half hours away, in Grant's Pass. From our jail cells we watched the coverage of our action on the evening news. The next morning, reporters for all the major newspapers were there, and we did more interviews for the television stations. We were released by Judge Kennedy, who banned us from returning to Bald Mountain or any other national forest.

We vowed to return anyway.

There would be dozens more protests and arrests during the Bald Mountain campaign. We finally got a good lawyer, Neil Kagan, and won a court victory stating that logging in roadless areas violated the Wilderness Act, setting a precedent to eventually protect several million acres of old growth.

The battle over Bald Mountain would prove to be historic but not decisive. To fight back, the timber industry and the Forest Service mounted a three-prong offensive against Earth First! First, they portrayed the group as violent radicals in an attempt to politically isolate us. Second, they would just ignore the law. The strategy was dependent on the hope that we would not have enough lawyers to appeal every timber sale. The third part of their approach was to use the criminal and civil courts to discourage activists from interfering with their operations. The courts threatened imposing jail terms and large fines.

Not long after we spiked the trees in Pyramid Creek, an article ran in the Albany, Oregon, paper. The wires picked up the story, and it went national. The next day, the story appeared in the *Wall Street Journal*. The headline read, WAR IN THE WOODS TURNS VIOLENT. It was a very sensational piece, playing up the dangers of tree spikes to the loggers. It was followed by articles in many more newspapers, and soon I was flying to places like New York and Los Angeles to do talk shows about tree spiking.

I was, of course, condemned not only by the timber industry, but by the leaders of the large environmental organizations as well. This was bad for the movement, I was told. But everywhere I went, people were winking and giving me the thumbs-up. While the main environmental groups hated to talk about tree spiking, the public wanted to hear more.

The sad fact was that our movement wasn't going anywhere. Our attempts at nonviolent civil disobedience were met with serious felony charges, expensive civil lawsuits against protesters, and violence from both police and timber workers. Most worrisome was that we could not get the media to drive out to these remote logging sites to cover our protests. It was simply too far to go to get footage of people sitting in front of bulldozers and logging trucks. It was a local story, and the local press was usually hostile.

Somehow, the *Wall Street Journal* article changed all of that. Frank Green, a reporter with NBC, called me the day the story came out. His editors had been dragging their feet for months on an article about old-growth forests. Now they pushed him to publish it.

"Mike," Frank said, "we in the news business often get accused of manufacturing the media, but when the *Journal* or the *Times* covers an issue—it's a story."

In the next few months, I did dozens more interviews on tree spiking. From all the call-in shows and interviews I did, two things became apparent. First, while not all Americans like tree spikers, they do like old growth forests, and they don't want them logged. Because of that, Earth First! did not have to be popular to be effective. Discussions about tree spiking were pushing the timber industry to justify its lousy record.

Two years later, I was riding north with Darryl Cherney along Highway 101. Cherney was a new Earth First! recruit from New York City. He was a musician and furniture mover with a wicked sense of humor, and someone with an almost spiritual connection to redwood forests ever since childhood. Over the last two years, he had been trying to revive the nascent forest campaign in Northern California in order to keep Charles Hurwitz and his Maxxam Corporation from logging off the state's last remaining stands of old-growth redwoods.

We were on our way to Garberville when we pulled over to get gas in the small town of Hopland. I grabbed a coffee and a newspaper.

Scanning the front page, I noticed a big headline: MILL WORKER INJURED BY TREE SPIKE.

"Judi's not going to like this," I said as I handed the paper to Darryl.

Indeed. Judi Bari was the Earth First! organizer at the Mendocino Environmental Center. A seasoned union organizer and red diaper baby from a leftist family in Baltimore, she had been on the scene since arriving in California ten years earlier.

We stopped in the Mendocino Environmental Center to check in and to call Judi.

"Of course they will blame it on Earth First!" she responded. "Who else would they blame it on?"

She was blaming this on me, so why wouldn't everybody else, I figured.

Sure enough, she was right. Soon the phones were ringing off the hook. We dashed up to Darryl's place, a sadly abandoned motel in Potter Valley, where we could work the phones. The injured mill worker, George Alexander, was on all the television networks. His head and shoulders were in bandages, and he was sitting with his new wife in a hospital bed. This was the handiwork of radical environmentalists, according to the timber industry and law enforcement. And there I was, on television, making statements supporting tree spiking. Another clip showed me getting hauled away by police on a logging road in Oregon.

The irony of this situation was that it did not have the hallmarks of an Earth First! tree spiking. None of the trees were old; they were second growth. None of the trees were in a roadless area or in critical wildlife habitat. They were spiked after they were felled, and most important, none of the logs were marked to indicate that they contained metal spikes. The Georgia-Pacific Lumber Company was aware of the spikes, had removed most of them, and was milling anyway, occasionally hitting one.

Alexander would later complain that the high-speed band saw had hit too many nails and was weakened. He mentioned to his wife that morning that he didn't want to operate the saw that day. He felt the company should shut down the line and replace it, because he thought it was going to break, which it did, with terrible consequences. Additionally, he didn't blame Earth First! but held the timber company responsible for the accident. Local rumors ran wild with speculation on who had actually spiked the tree. One suspect in the spiking was a local landowner, a conservative Republican. Legend had it that he was upset when the winter rains washed sediment off the logged slopes and onto the road. The ensuing mud made it slippery, causing him to drive off the road in his car.

Regardless of the lack of Earth First! involvement in the Hopland mill accident, the injury of George Alexander would make it impossible to support tree spiking in the future. If tree spiking had helped promote interest in the fate of the ancient forests, it was not going to get additional support now. We were facing a major PR disaster, and yet once more, I was doing interviews about tree spiking for reporters as far away as Scotland and Australia. I had to walk a fine line between standing up for my earlier statements and emphasizing that the campaign in the redwoods was nonviolent. It wasn't an easy task, nor do I suspect I was very convincing.

At a meeting in Eugene in 1990, I was finally convinced that when it came to tree spiking, we must declare a cease-fire. Judi Bari and Darryl Cherney insisted that tree spiking be renounced by Earth First! in order for them to participate in the upcoming Redwood Summer Campaign. We all signed a declaration to that effect.

At the time, it seemed that the signing of the tree spike treaty would stop the violence. But violence was brewing in the mountains and valleys of the Northwest. Mills were being shut down by a barrage of lawsuits paralyzing the Forest Service bureaucracy, and the campaign to save the last remnants of redwoods was heating up. The timber war was at a boiling point. And Judi Bari and Daryl Cherney were soon to be victims of a car bomb.

7

Redwood Summer and the Bombing of Judi Bari

When the bomb went off, everything changed.

I was driving up Interstate 5 with Mike Howell. It was May 24, 1990. California was green, and spring brought high water, so we were taking a few days off to run a river in Oregon. Unaware of the blast, we steered his lime green VW bus into the driveway of Michelle Miller's house in Chico.

Michelle was wholesome, attractive, passionate—and a national organizer for Redwood Summer. Like Judi, she had been receiving anonymous death threats through the mail. Howell and I wanted to see how she was holding up and give her a report from the Redwood Summer organizing meeting we had attended the night before in Oakland.

As soon as we pulled up to the house, Michelle came running out the front door in her nightgown. Her face was white and tense. Howell and I jumped out of the rig.

"Judi and Darryl have been bombed!" she shouted.

I was stunned, and stood staring at her, my mouth agape.

"They've been arrested by the Oakland police," Michelle continued. "The cops say the bomb was theirs. That's total bullshit. I've been doing damage control all morning. The San Francisco office is jammed, and they want you to stay here to work the phones."

When the explosion ripped through Judi's Subaru, she and Darryl were driving down an Oakland side street. The bomb, located directly under the driver's seat and equipped with a motion-activated switch, sent shrapnel consisting of hundreds of nails through Judi's pelvis and legs. Darryl escaped serious injury, but was badly shaken up. Both were taken to the prison ward of the Alameda County Medical Center and placed under guard. Both were being labeled by the FBI as terrorists.

Within minutes of the explosion, the scene of the blast was sealed off by FBI agents and the Oakland Police Department. Seizing a cardboard box from the wreckage, the FBI placed a charge next to it and set off a second explosion. The box had contained only Cherney's collection of environmental-music cassettes, but the dramatic footage of this explosion was rebroadcast repeatedly on local television during the next week.

In spite of the evidence the FBI claimed to have, it simply was not possible for Judi or Darryl to have made the bomb. Neither of them knew anything about explosives, or even owned a gun. Both were equally committed to keeping their campaigns nonviolent. Still, I was worried Judi and Darryl would disappear into the depths of the federal criminal justice system and that it would take years, even decades, to get them out. The FBI was acting quickly to frame the victims as the perpetrators, and to close the case.

The bombing came on the eve of Judi's brainchild—

Redwood Summer. She took her inspiration from Freedom Summer, the 1964 voting rights campaign that brought hundreds of volunteers into the Deep South to challenge segregation. The problems Earth First! was facing were similar to those of the civil rights movement in Mississippi. After six years of civil disobedience in the forests, we were running out of steam. Most of our activists had been arrested, many of them several times. We had been hit with lawsuits, there was increasing violence by loggers at the blockades, and we simply could not recruit enough people from the region for the amount of work needed to be done to win the campaign. We were at a turning point. The last large unprotected groves of redwoods would either be saved in the next few years or hastily logged to avoid looming forest protections.

Redwood Summer wasn't even officially named before the timber industry learned the details. They sent spies to our concept meetings and then completely overreacted. The airwaves were rife with warnings of violence toward Earth Firsters if anyone attempted to bring in protesters from out of state for a Redwood Summer.

Shortly thereafter, the Humboldt County sheriff announced that he didn't have enough jail cells or law enforcement for Redwood Summer. The Sierra Club and the Save the Redwoods League came out in opposition to the campaign. The county began complaining about how much the protest was going to cost and wondering how they were going to pay for it.

We were taxed for funds, too. The past six years had exhausted our bank account. Federal agents had stepped up pressure on the marijuana growers, and the north coast of California was beginning to look like occupied territory. The shock to the local economy from this loss of revenue had affected everyone, and our ability to raise money was also hampered. To clear Judi and Darryl and pull off Redwood Summer, we needed allies, and we needed them quick.

There was only one way to counter the terrorism charges. The first thing that had to be done was to get Judi and Darryl out of jail so they could begin to defend themselves. From Michelle's house in Chico, I decided that the media calls could wait. I picked up the phone and called Peter Bahouth, who had just become the executive director of Greenpeace. He was my boss when I was the action team coordinator, and he was chair of the Greenpeace board.

I knew Peter could provide invaluable advice. Shortly before he was hired to lead Greenpeace, that organization's flagship, the *Rainbow Warrior*, was bombed in the harbor of Auckland, New Zealand, by the French secret police. They were trying to prevent the ship from participating in antinuclear protests at the French nuclear testing site in Moruroa Atoll.

In the confusion surrounding the blast that sank the *Rainbow Warrior* and killed Greenpeace photographer Fernando Pereira, the French attempted to place the blame on Greenpeace. They said Greenpeace was carrying the bomb into the nuclear test site. Despite Greenpeace's record as an organization dedicated to nonviolence, many people bought into the distortions. After all, governments don't lie, do they?

Almost immediately after the bombing, France issued a statement denying involvement. "The French Government doesn't deal with its opponents in such ways," the press release asserted. In the days that followed the bombing of the *Rainbow Warrior*, two French secret service agents were arrested and charged with the bombing. There were implications that the order had come from France's President Francois Mitterrand.

Eventually the defense minister and an admiral took the rap for the bombing.

I did my best to explain our current situation as Peter listened silently. After a brief pause, Pete spoke. "Mike, I hope you understand, but I have to ask you one question." There was another pause. "Is there any chance that it was their bomb?"

"Absolutely not!" was my immediate reply.

"Okay. I promise I will never ask you that question again."

"Pete, we have to get them out of jail," I demanded. "They have to be able to answer to the charges themselves. They need to get their version of the events out there while there is still time to change the perception that they are dangerous terrorists."

At this point, Peter offered to do what he could. He put his entire organization to the task of supporting Judi and Darryl and came up with the one-million-dollar bail fee. Greenpeace also weighed in behind the Redwood Summer Campaign, lending all the resources that the world's largest environmental organization could muster.

After posting bail the next morning, Darryl Cherney was released from the hospital with his ears still ringing from the blast. Judi Bari was moved to the intensive care unit of the hospital. Meanwhile, Bahouth and Friends of the Earth executive director Michael Clark had gotten the major environmental groups like the Sierra Club and Audubon Society to close ranks behind Judi, demanding that the terrorism charges be dropped. Similar support was coming in from environmental groups around the country, a dividend from Judi and Darryl's tireless efforts to build support for protecting the redwood forests over the past three years.

Slowly, the tide was turning.

The fact of the matter is that the bomb was placed in Judi's car to stop Redwood Summer. And what happened is that the bombing brought more attention than ever to the plight of the redwoods.

Within moments of Judi and Darryl's arrest, calls poured into our offices from around the country, offering money and help. Within a week, there were seven separate offices opened in California alone, and other offices around the country, including New York City. A field camp was established to receive the volunteers flooding in from all corners of the country. Judi may have been in the hospital with a severely damaged pelvis, but the campaign she worked so hard to launch was pushing forward and was now being covered by the international news media.

The field camp was set up outside Petrolia, a small coastal town in Humboldt County. I arrived at the camp on a hot afternoon. The place was bustling with activity. There were people sitting in large circles, having long-winded meetings. There was a small group teaching new recruits to climb trees, and another group rigging cement-filled barrels with chains to form barricades.

People bathed nude in the creek, and of course, the drums were beating. The drums first appeared at the initial redwood protests at Maxxam's Pacific Lumber office in the San Francisco financial district. The drummers didn't want to march or chant; they said they just wanted to provide good energy. Now there were hundreds of them, and it was hard to get any sleep in the camp.

I had never seen this many hippies in one place without a band playing. Some people were referring to this as Redwoodstock, and everywhere was the smell of the sweet local sinsemilla and the sight of young well-tanned youth—naked and dreadlocked—all getting ready for direct action.

Not everyone was young. As I took in the scene, I was approached by an older man with a well-trimmed beard and short hair, almost completely gray.

"I heard about the bombing while I was living in L.A.," he said. "I was thinking about retiring from my job as a life insurance salesman, so I decided to come up here and spend the summer with Earth First! in the redwoods."

The man doing the talking was Robert Amon. In a few days, he would be arrested for the first time in his life. Afterwards, Amon sold his house, bought an old school bus, equipped it with a kitchen, bunks for six, and dedicated himself to driving around, feeding activists who were trying to save the planet.

Redwood Summer was to be one of those campaigns. Nothing like this had ever happened before. Now everyone was getting into the act. At one point, the owners of a local bed-and-breakfast set up a full champagne buffet in the middle of the road to prevent the loggers from getting to work. The first day, the loggers had coffee and chatted amiably with their caterers. The next morning, they rammed their truck through the buffet line, as their hosts dived for the ditches on the side of the road. Similar skirmishes were occurring wherever the industry attempted to log the remaining old groves of redwoods.

The summer rolled on, and thousands of young activists converged on the redwoods in a series of demonstrations against logging that were the largest this country has ever seen. Many hundreds were arrested. Roads were blocked. Trees were climbed. Hippies chained themselves to bulldozers, log trucks, and just about anything they could get a U-lock around. Additionally, lawsuits were being filed and logging was coming to a halt one redwood grove at a time.

The most important exception to this was in the heart of

redwood country, the largest unprotected forest in the state: the Headwaters Forest. Headwaters had recently been purchased by a savings-and-loan corporate raider from Texas, Charles Hurwitz. Using funds from a savings-and-loan bank that later collapsed, Hurwitz engaged in a hostile takeover of the Pacific Lumber Company. Then he drained the worker pension fund and nearly tripled the rate of logging in the world's largest stand of privately held ancient redwood forest.

It should be criminal not to stop a man like Hurwitz. But, most people can't imagine standing out of line. Even here in America, there's a chance you could get car-bombed, then have the government call you a terrorist.

The Oakland police, succumbing to a pressure campaign that was growing by the day, eventually dropped charges against the two activists for possession of an explosive device. Bari and Cherney fought the FBI in court until Judi's death in 1997 from breast cancer, adamantly claiming they were falsely arrested with fabricated evidence in an effort to damage reputations.

In 2002, an Oakland jury sided with Cherney and the late Judi Bari. It took twelve years, but a jury ordered four FBI agents and three Oakland police officers to pay up $4.4 million for violation of Judi and Darryl's First Amendment rights to speak and organize, and for false arrest and unlawful search and seizure.

In 2003, the Oakland City Council unanimously voted a resolution saying,

Whereas, Judi Bari was a dedicated activist, who worked for many social and environmental causes, the most prominent being the protection and stewardship of California's ancient redwood forests . . . Whereas, on May 24, 1990, Judi Bari was the victim of a car bombing in Oakland that nearly took her life; Now therefore be it resolved that the City of Oakland shall designate May 24 as Judi Bari Day and celebrate and honor the work of Judi Bari in advancing the causes of forest protection, eco-feminism, labor organizing, bridge building between environmentalists and timber workers, and civil rights for political activists; And be it further resolved that the City shall encourage its schools, civic institutions and citizens to memorialize Judi Bari's work through art, media, festivals, school assignments and other creative means.

The public is fickle, and oftentimes blind. Judi was condemned by this community as a terrorist a decade earlier. Now schoolkids are encouraged to mimic her activism.

To this day, people still argue over whether Redwood Summer was a success or a failure. Most criticism cites the failure of environmentalists to pass a Big Green ballot measure. By this time, the stereotypical Northern California tree hugger had become a caricature, associated with dreadlocks and sinsemilla. Earth First!, in the process, morphed from a small group of activists to a national organization that no longer wanted to be defined by the antics of its founders. Being a big dog came with advantages and disadvantages. New Earth First! groups were springing up like mushrooms after a spring rain. There were even groups in Poland, the Czech Republic, and Russia.

After Redwood Summer, a statewide referendum called the Forests Forever Initiative was put to ballot. The Forests Forever Initiative called for protection for all California old growth. Activists hit the streets and gathered thousands of signatures. The campaign spent over a million dollars just to get the measure on the ballot. The timber industry had a right, by law, to put their side of the argument on the ballot information pamphlet. In their arguments, they referred to it as the Earth First! Initiative and falsely claimed it was written by radical environmentalists. The sponsors of the bill were horrified. Because the bombing case was still under investigation, and because of the ruckus that had been created by thousands of protesters converging on the small towns along the coast, they had no desire to be identified with Earth First! Naturally, Forests Forever lawyers took the Western Forest Products Alliance to court to have the language changed.

Darryl Cherney and I were called as witnesses, both by the prosecution and by the defense. The Forests Forever coalition argued that since Earth First! was not an organization, but rather a movement, it couldn't endorse the initiative and it clearly didn't write it. The timber-industry lawyers argued that Earth First! was an organization, and that the initiative language mirrored proposals published in the *Earth First! Journal*.

So here I was, sitting in an ornate Sacramento courtroom, listening to high-priced lawyers on each side arguing whether Earth First! was a movement or an organization. I had witnessed these very arguments at Earth First! meetings many times, and I, of course, knew that by the letter of the law, Earth First! certainly was an organization with bank accounts, officers, equipment, computers, and lists of supporters. The judge ended up ruling with the timber industry, and the language remained unchanged. The argument within Earth First! on whether it is an organization or a movement still continues today.

The timber industry launched a two-million-dollar campaign against Forests Forever. A television ad featuring a young forest ranger saying she would be unable to put out fires if the law was enacted was particularly effective.

The initiative went down in flames.

Because of this setback, many conservationists began to view Redwood Summer as an unmitigated disaster. Earth First! co-founder Dave Foreman resigned from the group in an angry letter to the *New York Times*, dismissing the California Earth Firsters as hippies, punks, and shoplifters. Foreman claimed that Earth First! had been taken over by socialists. Foreman's resignation was hailed by the timber industry in Northern California, who saw this as proof that Earth First! was too radical even for its founder. Foreman, meanwhile, was in the midst of his own battle with the FBI.

The accusation that Judi was a socialist and that she was more concerned for the local economy than she was about wilderness is simply not backed up by the facts. True, she tried to enlist timber workers into the cause, but she was unwilling to compromise even one redwood to gain their support. As a result, very few loggers were part of the coalition. Nevertheless, Judi believed there was a future for logging if the rate of harvest was reduced, and if old-growth groves were protected with adequate buffer zones. Although opposed violently by the timber industry, it certainly wasn't a radical position.

It would be the string of successful lawsuits by the Garberville-based Environmental Protection and Information Center (EPIC) that would result in a prohibition on logging in many of the remaining old-growth redwood groves.

Still, the Headwaters Campaign would continue for another ten years, and there would be many more demonstrations, blockades, tree sits, and hundreds of arrests, including a dramatic climb of the Golden Gate Bridge by actor Woody Harrelson and others, as well as arrests of Bonnie Raitt, Don Henley, and many musicians and other celebrities.

Finally, in 2007, Pacific Lumber filed for bankruptcy, and Charles Hurwitz lost control of the company. Mendocino Redwood Company purchased the company and plans to protect the old-growth forests and reduce cutting on former Pacific Lumber holdings.

Meanwhile in Idaho, another battle was brewing, this time in one in the most remote wilderness areas outside of Alaska: the greater Salmon-Selway. Unlike the redwoods, the area surrounding the Cove/Mallard timber sale was not close to any populated areas, had few local supporters, a very hostile citizenry, and was virtually unknown. Only a few hunters, the U.S. Forest Service's timber cruisers, and a few lonely conservationists knew about this last tract of untrammeled land.

One retired insurance salesman with a well-trimmed beard and an old school bus was about to change all of that forever.

8

Holding Idaho's High Ground—A Decade in Cove/Mallard

Redwood Summer was the largest grassroots forest campaign since the 1960s. The campaign to save the redwoods hosted some of the largest demonstrations and mass arrests since the height of the Vietnam War. While there was still a lot to be done, some nomadic Earth First! activists started to cast their gaze at work to be done elsewhere.

By November of 1990, we had pretty much rolled up the whole Redwood Summer operation. The students and itinerant activists had gone home. The field offices in Arcata and Garberville were vacated. The computers, radios, and fax machines were returned to Greenpeace. Bills were paid. The campaign was on solid footing. I began to long for a change of scenery. That change was only a phone call away.

I called Peter Bahouth, the executive director of Greenpeace.

Bahouth had helped us out by raising the bail money for Judi Bari and Darryl Cherney. I owed him. He offered me a job, and I could not really refuse an assignment. I made one request. I asked that he not send me to Las Vegas. Greenpeace was organizing a massive antinuclear rally at the gates of the Nevada Test Site. The rally would include two hundred Kazakhs opposing Russian nuclear-weapons testing in the deserts of Kazakhstan.

"I'm ready to come to Washington if the job's still available," I said.

"Yeah, I could still use your help here in D.C.," he said. "I want to create a rapid-response team for Greenpeace. But first, I have a job for you."

"So, what's the job?" I asked.

"I want you to go to Nevada," he replied.

The reasons I didn't want to work in Nevada were twofold. One, having spent many months in Las Vegas on the campaign since 1986, including two stints in jail, I did not relish going back to Vegas and working for months out of a cheap motel room. The second reason was that my girlfriend, Claire Greensfelder, had just been hired to coordinate the Greenpeace Nuke campaign. She would be my boss.

There were pluses, though. Seeds of Peace had just completed its support work on the Redwood Summer campaign and was hired by Greenpeace to coordinate logistics. I'd be working closely with Seeds. They had rented an abandoned church in North Las Vegas and set up a headquarters. I headed for Nevada and set up a post in the church so I wouldn't have to live in the motel.

The Nevada team had entered crisis mode when I arrived. Greenpeace was planning a mega-event. It was now way over budget, and costs had to be cut. This included reducing the Kazakh contingent from two hundred to twenty, causing discontent amongst the Kazakhstan delegation. We would end up with ten of the leading Kazakh potentates and their mistresses. My job was to be their guide. Claire, who spoke some Russian, was the interpreter. This arrangement worked well until the delegates wanted to be taken to the strip clubs and porno shops downtown. In this endeavor, they were on their own.

Some two thousand protesters showed up for the rally, including two hundred nurses in town for a large convention. A small group of the nurses wanted to be arrested blocking the gate. Already there were several groups of this size participating, including a Greenpeace group and a celebrity group that included Carl Sagan, Kris Kristofferson, Martin Sheen, and Robert Blake, among others.

The evening before the protest, Robert Blake walked into the motel room that served as our media office. "Can I ask you guys a question?"

"Sure," I said. "What do you want to know?"

"Do you guys pray at your meetings?" Blake inquired.

"Well, no," I responded cautiously, unsure where he was going with the questioning.

"Do you hold hands in a circle and sing a lot of songs together?" he continued.

"Definitely not!" I responded, now more confidently.

"In that case, can I get arrested with you guys?"

"Here, have a beer! And just meet us at the gate of the test site in the morning."

For its part in the action, Greenpeace was going to launch a hot-air balloon and attempt to parachute a former English commando into ground zero. This plan was abandoned when his parachute was confiscated on his flight to the test site. As a result, we had a loud, extremely obnoxious, self-aggrandizing adventurer in our midst with nothing to do but insult the women and regale the men with tales of his manly exploits.

The day of the protest was clear and crisp, with a slight breeze from the east. The crowd was estimated to be around two thousand people. We launched the balloon, minus the commando. The pilot was able to bring it down just across the cattle guard into the test site and into the midst of a large force of military-police officers. Wackenhut private security officers and Nye County sheriff's deputies were waiting for the touch-down.

Afterwards, we crossed the cattle guard en masse, and I was jailed with Blake and eight hundred other activists. After being released, I got back into my VW van and drove to Washington, D.C., to look for an apartment with Claire and work with Peter to assemble a rapid-response team for Greenpeace.

A year earlier, I had separated from my wife, Karen Pickett. Karen was a key San Francisco Bay Area organizer for Redwood Summer. She had started an Earth First! group back in 1982, and also worked at the Ecology Center in Berkeley on local environmental issues. Claire was also well established in Bay Area political circles, a key fund-raiser in the campaign, and had pulled many strings for Judi and Darryl. Claire even got Darryl and me a meeting with Oakland's mayor, Elihu Harris. Here, Darryl was able to personally make his case to the boss of the Oakland police and the prosecutors who were charging him with terrorism. Terrorism charges naturally create unhappy situations. Because of this history, I was glad to escape the cloud hanging over the West Coast. I was heading East for a while.

For a year, I was to lead the new Greenpeace Rapid Response Team, a special-operations group that would report directly to the executive director. The team could deploy quickly, working outside the normal Greenpeace planning process, which had grown more political and bureaucratic in the preceding years.

Peter wanted to introduce reforms that would make the organization more flexible, but before he had time to implement any new programs, the Gulf War broke out. For the next six months, Greenpeace would be too distracted by its antiwar efforts to expend any energy on reforms.

The bureaucracy remained in place. Peter came under fire when donations to Greenpeace plummeted, necessitating extreme budget-cutting measures, including the layoff of half the paid staff. The resulting upheaval resulted in both Peter and me losing our jobs. And, given that we were on opposite sides in the budgetary battles, it was also the beginning of the end of my relationship with Claire.

I flew back to Grants Pass, Oregon, to disappear into the Siskiyou wilderness for a while and contemplate my next move.

During November of 1991, there was a rare winter meeting of the national Earth First! leadership in an old, moldy Civilian Conservation Corps camp outside of Portland. By this time, Judi Bari was well enough to attend. Relying on a walker to get around and suffering from intense pain, she refused any pain medication. Judi had become the voice of a growing new force in Earth First! This faction was demanding more say in the direction of the movement. They were no longer amused by the redneck, beer-drinking image of the original Buckaroos.

The Californians were especially concerned about the reputation for misogyny and racism that had resulted from some of Foreman's more rabid writings. Two years earlier, they had scored what they perceived as a major victory when Foreman resigned and the *Earth First! Journal* was moved to Missoula, Montana, to be run by a more or less neutral faction of the organization. It was not long, however, before even the Montana location was deemed unsatisfactory by the new Progressive wing of activists in California and Oregon. According to Judi, the office was a nest of spies and provocateurs and she was prepared to go to the mat to clean it out.

I watched all of this unfold with amusement. I had been out of the picture for a year, and was unwilling to commit to either side of the debate. Especially since my ex-wife Karen was part of the contingent that was calling for the heads of the Missoula staff. I was sympathetic to the Montana position, and the staff included many personal friends, none of whom could possibly be an FBI agent. Unfortunately, my reticence was mistaken for impartiality. After a long meeting, which I did not attend, I was chosen to be the new editor of the twelve-year-old *Earth First! Journal*.

I was instructed by Judi to clean out the nest of spies and provocateurs in Missoula, and handed a Greyhound bus ticket. My salary was fifty dollars a month. But, I could sleep in the office above a very bad Chinese restaurant in downtown Missoula.

I arrived in Missoula the day after the Oregon meeting. I was accompanied by Tim Bechtold. Tim had been the only member of the *Journal* staff, and the only Montanan present at the meeting. He hadn't had time to report back to Missoula. The Missoulians would be getting the news that I had been chosen as the new editor, without their consent, upon our arrival.

The first meeting was tense until I explained that Judi had sent me to clean out this nest of infiltrators. I warned them that I would be watching them closely. Surprisingly, nobody quit, and we were able to keep putting out a good newspaper that covered a range of issues without undue interference. One issue we covered closely was the roadless issue. One roadless area we focused on would come to be known as Cove/Mallard.

Roadless areas were on the chopping block in the spring of '92. No region faced more wide-scale destruction, or had more to lose, than wild Idaho's rugged temperate rain forests. While several timber sales were planned for Montana's roadless areas, there were also several environmental groups responding to the intrusions. Meanwhile, central Idaho didn't have a single Earth First! group. Wild Rockies Earth First! decided it would be a good idea to drive over the pass from Missoula and draw some attention to a controversial plan to log in the heart of the little-known Greater Salmon-Selway Ecosystem, the largest roadless area in the Lower 48.

The Cove/Mallard campaign started with an article in the *Earth First! Journal* written by Steve Paulson, a third-generation farmer from Idaho, and Phil Knight, an Earth Firster from Bozeman. After Paulson and Knight walked the areas proposed for logging by the Forest Service, they declared the plan a disastrous blow for roadless areas and biodiversity. They were pleading for help from anyone who would listen. Nobody had ever heard of Cove/Mallard or had been there, but we agreed to help. Little did we know that we were launching a seven-year campaign that would forever change how the Forest Service managed roadless areas.

Boy, oh boy, this was some timber sale! It was Big Wild versus Industrial Forestry.

Formally named as the Jersey-Jack timber sale, the project

had been so controversial that the Forest Service withdrew the proposal following an appeal by Walt Minnick, the former owner of the famed Selway River Whitewater Ranch. Minnick was no radical tree hugger. Instead, he ran Trus-Joist Mac-Millan, a large timber venture. But, he understood the value the area possessed beyond its lumber.

What eventually became known as Cove/Mallard, named for nearby Cove Mountain and Big and Little Mallard Creeks, was perched between three large wilderness areas and nestled deep in the region of Idaho known as the Greater Salmon-Selway Ecosystem. That ecosystem ranges from Lake Coeur D'Alene in the north to Idaho City in the south, and from the Snake River in the west to the Bitterroot Mountains of Montana in the east.

Cove/Mallard is central to this immense region and provides critical habitat for a host of species like the bull trout, chinook salmon, steelhead, fisher, marten, lynx, wolverine, gray wolf, bald eagle, and northern goshawk. Many of these species were endangered or threatened because of logging and road-building activities. The gray wolf had been exterminated from the area years earlier. But Cove/Mallard was part of an area that had been identified as key to the wolf's recovery. The necessity of their reintroduction to the area had been advocated by environmentalists for years. And though the feds wouldn't admit it, top biologists suspected that a few secretive grizzly bears were living in the ecosystem, though they, too, had been officially exterminated years earlier. Locals also claimed to have seen occasional gray wolves in Cove/Mallard.

Cove/Mallard's inventoried roadless area contained seventy-seven thousand acres of dense coniferous forest, and was an unprotected beating heart, centered between three of the largest protected wilderness areas in the contiguous United States. The region was and is a vital biological corridor for the area's wildlife that travel between the Frank Church River of No Return Wilderness (2.2 million acres), the Selway-Bitterroot Wilderness (1.3 million acres), and the Gospel Hump Wilderness (400,000 acres).

This was to be the largest timber sale in the history of the Forest Service's Region One, and one of the costliest for taxpayers. Due to the remote, roadless terrain, it was certain to be one of the largest deficit timber sales on the agency's books. That means building the roads for a private corporation to profit off logging public land was going to cost taxpayers a lot of money.

Upon fully assessing all of this, Wild Rockies Earth First! decided to mount a vigorous campaign. We sent out a press release, and when Tim Bechtold got the call at the Earth First! office from a lone Idaho reporter, she wanted to know what we were going to do.

"A Viking thing," he replied.

When he hung up, I looked over from my computer and said, "What is a Viking thing?"

"The supervisor's name is Mike King," Tim replied. "We'll dress up as Vikings and shout 'Death to the King!'"

The Nez Perce National Forest Headquarters is in Grangeville, Idaho, known regionally as Strangeville. Strangeville is located on the Camas Prairie high above the Salmon River and the South Fork of the Clearwater on Idaho's western border. The Forest Service headquarters is a low-slung, nondescript concrete bunker built on the edge of town. We had no problem scaling the roof with our ladders. Equipped with cardboard swords and shields, we began chanting for the King!

Sure enough, out came the forest supervisor, Mike King. We sent Steve Paulson down to negotiate with the King. Our negotiator had filed numerous appeals and lawsuits against the Forest Service. In fact, few people knew the rules and regulations better than he. Before long, the King was on the defensive. That was easy to achieve, because of one simple fact: This massive and intrusive timber sale was illegal.

A picture of King arguing with the Vikings appeared in the local paper. We didn't know it at the time, but a new timber war was getting ready to break out.

Before I continue this story, it is necessary for anyone who doesn't live in logging country—that is, most of us—to understand the psychology of a timber town. I have always argued that forestry is a religion, and not a science. No amount of science will convince a logger, a forester, a timber executive, or a United States Forest Ranger that clear-cut logging is bad for the environment and bad for business. True, after the trees are gone and the mill is shut down, some loggers will agree that mistakes were made, but never by them. It was always the government or the company's fault. Yet, if there is even one sawmill still in operation in a community, any critic of logging will be taking their life into their own hands.

I'd been warned plenty of times. While living in Jackson, Wyoming, I had become involved in a fight against a timber sale in Dubois, which borders the Bridger-Teton National Forest. Or, as Howie Wolke called it, the Louisiana-Pacific National Forest, named after the owners of one of the largest mills in Dubois.

"Why cut timber here? The slopes are steep, the soils thin, the growing season short. You could get more timber from one section in Oregon or Washington than you can get out of this entire county," Howie argued, unafraid. He was an exception. The atmosphere of intimidation created an environment where few stood against plans to log in the wilderness. Those few who tried were run out of town by angry loggers, in fear of their safety, after every public hearing on protecting roadless areas.

Later, traveling to Oregon to oppose old-growth logging, I heard the same things from local conservationists.

"Mike, this isn't some ski town in the Rockies. You are in Oregon. It's different here," one activist would say. Indeed. In those days in Oregon, conservationists argued that it made no sense to log the old growth.

"The slopes are too steep, the soils are too fragile, and logging the ancient forest is bad for wildlife. You can't grow trees like a plantation in the Coast Range," another activist would say. "You can grow trees more profitably on the southeastern pine plantations where the ground is flat and the growing season's longer."

Still, they did not propose ending the practice of clear-cutting on public lands. No, they wanted to protect only a few of the high-profile groves and roadless areas, remaining silent on the fate of the forests outside their immediate area of concern. Nevertheless, the timber industry responded by labeling these conservationists as radical—even violent—anti-capitalists. It was ironic because so far the conservationists were the only victims of violence.

The next year I was in East Texas, where the Forest Service was busy logging oak, hickory, and other hardwoods in one of the few small wilderness areas in the state, called the Four Notch. After the logging, they planned to use napalm delivered by helicopters to burn everything that did not make it to the mill. Then they would plant fast-growing loblolly pines for paper pulp. I am not making this up.

The Forest Service has long been a master of newspeak and distortion. Forestry is complicated and easy to construe. The official reason the Forest Service offered for the napalm attack was that the forest was in danger of being infested by pine bark beetles, which don't attack hardwoods. Another favorite Forest Service rationale was that the old trees might fall over and kill someone. Here conservationists demanded only that their small remnant hardwood forest, remaining in a two-million-acre sea of pines, be spared for the benefit of the endangered red-cockaded woodpecker.

"You're not in Oregon, Mike," local activists said. "This is East Texas. Georgia-Pacific is the largest landowner, largest employer, and owns all the politicians here."

Here, too, conservationists lived in fear, even seeking to preempt any federal endangered-species regulations that would arouse the ire of the locals. Loggers were shooting any red-cockaded woodpecker they encountered on the job.

"If you see a peckerwood tree, cut it down first, before anyone else knows about it," one logger told me. Of course, the truth is that logging communities have always been dangerous for conservationists. Speak out at a public hearing, and your dog will be shot or poisoned, roofing nails may be thrown on your driveway, your car windows shot out, and your children harassed at school. You can experience all of this even if you generally support the logging industry, and just want a few tiny wilderness areas off-limits to logging.

It is easy to see why loggers would see conservationists as a threat to their livelihoods, even when it is the timber companies that are liquidating the forest that logging jobs depend on.

It should be no surprise that loggers have an almost religious faith in their right to log. For over one hundred years, the timber industry, through the "scientific discipline" of forestry, has preached the gospel of sustained yield. The proponents of sustained yield argue that since a forest grows at a predictable rate, foresters should be able to harvest a sustainable amount of timber as long as they don't exceed that rate.

While this claim seems logical at first glance, it has a serious flaw: If you begin with a section of ancient forest—that is, trees in excess of four hundred years old—you start with a high-volume forest, one that has a staggering amount of standing biomass. Remove the thick, ancient trees and plant new little skinny ones. Now you have a low-volume forest, even though it may contain ten times the number of trees. Let those grow twenty years for pulp. Or forty years for saw logs. Either way, you still have a low-volume forest with minimal standing biomass, especially when compared with the four-hundred-year-old forest that was present at the beginning. At this point, you clear-cut again, causing even more soil depletion, possibly preventing even a single tree from ever growing on that site again. How is that sustainable?

The only way it can be considered sustainable is if from this point on, a regular and predictable amount of timber could be cut in perpetuity. This, too, sounds logical. We sacrificed an ancient forest rich in wildlife, complete with yet undiscovered species, and replaced it with a mono crop, but at least we will have a regular supply of lumber in which to build our homes.

Unfortunately, the logic is seriously and fatally flawed. Having taken thousands of tons of biomass off the forest floor, and having exposed it to harsh sunlight, heat, and drying winds, the soils that were once protected by the forest canopy start to decompose and lose their productivity. After another cut or two, the soils are impoverished. Yields will be successively lowered. Nothing has been sustained but the stubborn belief by foresters that the next time we log an ancient forest, things will be different, and the forest will actually regrow into something resembling the original. This has never happened, chiefly because foresters rarely follow their own rules. No industry has ever been more corrupt than the timber industry, which has never been successfully regulated.

Not even the Romans could enforce their forestry laws, and because of that failure, they eventually ran short of timber and water. The reason for a belief in the supernatural abilities of forests to withstand heavy logging goes back to the creation of the forest industry during the dawn of history. One can imagine Gilgamesh telling the locals that logging the ancient cedars would create jobs without harming the environment. Those forests disappeared before the Greeks began to write philosophy.

Later, medieval foresters, by taking a long view, actually came close to achieving sustained yield, primarily because they wished to leave a profitable business to their heirs. Above all, medieval foresters recognized that a healthy forest had many benefits, timber being but one of them. For the medieval forester, hunting, fishing, and other forms of food-gathering were essential, and the gathering of medicinal herbs also profitable. Still, these forests, some still producing timber today, were established at the expense of the ancient forests, which, by the time the Middle Ages came to a close and the Renaissance had begun, had almost totally disappeared from Europe.

We generally credit Gifford Pinchot, the founder of the U.S.

Forest Service, as introducing sustained yield as the guiding principle of American forestry. Pinchot's motto, "The greatest good for the greatest number," was belied by the fact that the Forest Service not only continued the cut-and-run policies of the pioneers, cloaking them in the mantle of sustainability, but also subsidized them with millions of dollars of U.S. taxpayer money. Areas so remote and so rugged that no timber company would invest in the roads and infrastructure to log them were now being liquidated for the sole purpose of keeping a few faltering sawmills in wood for another decade or so. At that point, the timber companies abandoned the communities altogether, as they had done before in so many other regions of the country.

These timber sales rarely, if ever, return the money invested in them, and are called deficit timber sales by the Forest Service. This simply means that the Forest Service offers the timber to the highest bidder, even if the cost of marking, logging, replanting, thinning, and regulating is never recovered. The Forest Service doesn't even factor in the value of a standing old-growth forest for wildlife, recreation, watershed protection, and fish habitat. Not to mention the economic value in forest products like mushrooms, berries, and medicinal herbs. These forest products alone are more valuable than the timber and can be harvested every year with little long-term impact. Ultimately, not only is a great deal of taxpayer money lost, but truly sustainable industries and their jobs are eliminated, as well.

Cove/Mallard was the Mother of All Deficit Timber Sales. When we started adding up all the area's unique characteristics: its remote location, the fact that it's encircled by the largest roadless area outside of Alaska, and that it borders the wild Salmon River canyon—we were mad!

The sheer size of the Salmon-Selway allows evolutionary processes to fully function, something that has been stopped virtually everywhere in the temperate world by industrialized human activity. Less than 5 percent of United States primary forest remains intact. By comparison, over 90 percent of the Salmon-Selway's forest remained unlogged—so far.

In Cove/Mallard, the strategy of the Forest Service was to build a network of 145 miles of new logging roads. Once the roads were in, nine timber sales would be carved into six thousand acres using two hundred clear-cuts. Bridges would be constructed. Gravel pits and logging decks would find their way into the pristine forest in order to allow the local timber company, Shearer Lumber, to get access to some of the largest and oldest trees left in Idaho.

It was another dumb Forest Service logging project designed to perpetuate the logging industry at a cost we could no longer afford. The law was being broken. Our job was to stop the Forest Service, along with the logging and road-building companies.

A few months later, an old hippie with gray hair and a beard, sporting a red bandanna for a headband, showed up at the Earth First! rendezvous in southwestern Colorado. He had a bus and a brigade of forest activists he'd recruited at Redwood Summer. I'd met this hippie before, only he had been a well-groomed retired insurance salesman. It was Ramon, reincarnated as an aging hippie. The Redwood Battle had changed him.

Ramon has always been famous for his letters. Even in the electronic age, he insisted on fastidiously punching out correspondence on his manual typewriter and then dropping the note in the mail. Call him old school. It was, in fact, his return address that earned him the name Ramon. He always marked the top left corner of the envelope with his name, R. Amon. Eventually it was shortened to Ramon.

In the early spring of 1992, Phil Knight received one of Ramon's famous letters. We got one at the *Earth First! Journal* office in Missoula, too. The letter read, "I bought a school bus, had it fixed up with a kitchen, and now I want to feed the hippies doing forest protest, except nobody is protesting. I read that you guys were going to try to stop the logging in Cove/Mallard. I thought I'd come up in the bus and see how I could help out."

We agreed to meet at the rendezvous in July of '92.

I had not seen Ramon since Redwood Summer and was shocked at his appearance. Gone was the dignified businessman. In his place was just another aging Rocky Mountain hippie.

"Ramon, lose the ponytail and the headband," I advised him. "Remember, you're a retired life-insurance salesman from Philadelphia, not some wannabe New Age shaman."

Reluctantly, Ramon took this advice and so ended his short career as a hippie. He set out for the small town of Dixie with his motley crew to set up camp deep in the wilderness. The Ancient Forest Bus Brigade consisted of Ramon; Catfish, a grizzled army vet; Cindy, who claimed to have been raised by bikers; Russell, a young lanky straight-edged kid from Florida; and Bones, Cindy's old, flea-bitten hound dog.

The Ancient Forest Bus Brigade was an unlikely group of activists for the task it had set for itself. The loggers in central Idaho had a reputation for violence beyond anything we'd ever encountered. We had not one ally in the region, with the state's few conservationists holed up safely in Boise, or in the resort towns of Stanley and Sun Valley. A few were working in the college town of Moscow. There were also small handfuls of lawyers trying to stop new timber sales from being approved. But there were too many timber sales to file against all of them, and in 1992, most of the legal challenges came from out-of-state attorneys in Montana, Washington, or San Francisco. Not one visible conservationist lived in Dixie, Elk City, Grangeville, or Kooskia.

A grassroots campaign was out of the question. Ramon discovered this quickly while risking his life polling the residents of Dixie. The only solution was to bring on the hippies to blockade the roads with their bodies, à la Redwood Summer, while we took the bastards to court! The question was, where would the hippies come from? Certainly not central Idaho. The few back-to-landers on the ground were not going to stick their necks out, with the exception of Steve Paulson. Although we were not yet despised by the locals, they were much too wary to publicly associate themselves with tree huggers. The only solution was to focus recruitment efforts on the college towns of Missoula and Moscow. The two towns were in different states, but they were equidistant to the Cove/Mallard timber sales. And, we would try to get a foothold in Boise.

Boise had always been a challenge for conservationists. It was the largest city in Idaho, but had few full-time conservationists. One of them was Ron Mitchell, director of the Idaho Sporting Congress. He had a small office in downtown Boise and was interested in the Cove/Mallard timber sale after being approached by Ramon and Steve Paulson. He was particularly interested in the loss of critical elk and big-game habitat. He was also concerned with the hit that the world-class salmon fishery would take due to sediment discharge after the construction of 145 miles of roads.

The filing of *Idaho Sporting Congress v. U.S. Forest Service* received scant notice at the time, but this action would prove to be a ticking time bomb as it wound its way through the courts.

After a series of preliminary actions and some arrests in 1992, including the first-ever tripod road blockade in North America, all hell broke loose in Cove/Mallard during the summer of '93. Steve Paulson suffered a broken jaw in an attack that was filmed by an ABC camera crew and appeared on the national news. At one point, in mid-July, several dozen activists blockaded the road. Four activists were buried chest deep in the road. Two tripods spanned above the road. One activist even locked herself to the chassis of the first Forest Service truck to reach the blockade.

The tripod was a favored tactical tool. It was constructed of three logs that were felled to build the road. The structure resembled a tepee frame and housed an activist locked into the apex of the impediment, thirty feet above the ground. Tripods were effective because only one person was needed to stop traffic for hours, sometimes even days, or months. Removing a hippie from a tripod is a tedious process if you are concerned about the person's safety. Of course, there were many instances where the extraction process was rushed and the sitter was placed in considerable harm.

We had nothing but time. The Idaho County sheriffs were located hours away. Once a road blockade was installed, it often took six or more hours just to get enough cops to try to reclaim the road. And we were not afraid of jail. On the contrary, Earth First! activists were in the Grangeville jail throughout the seven-year campaign. A few even thought the food was better than at camp.

Thus began the war of attrition. The Freddies were up against a very tenacious group of hippies who had very little to lose, except the forest itself. With the blockades being impossible to predict, without enough officers in the county to guard the road, and with even fewer Forest Service law enforcement officers, the loggers felt exposed and unprotected. They were constantly looking over their shoulder, never knowing when we might impede the operation.

They intimidated us. We intimidated them. Rick Valois and the Eco Rangers, complete with military uniforms, volunteered to guard the road and our camp against any attacks from the loggers. Rick liked to carry a sidearm. Ramon said they could patrol the road, but maintained that no guns or other weapons could be taken into camp, which was now on a twenty-acre former mining claim he had purchased outside of Dixie. Ramon insisted that the cops obey his no-gun rule, too. The Eco Rangers quickly tired of marching up and down the road and disappeared, but their impact would linger.

Law-enforcement costs, including private security that the road-builder Highland Construction hired, exceeded $2 million that year alone. The price would continue to rise, along with the cost of the civil litigation, which at this point Highland's owner Don Blewett had decided was the only way to stop us.

As soon as the blockades went up in '93, the Forest Service and the FBI responded in force. Ramon's camp was raided in the middle of the night. All their possessions—including ad-

dress books, tools, tents, plane tickets, and even Catfish's cook-
ing pots—were confiscated.

Tensions mounted. The loggers were losing patience. Dozens of activists were being arrested. By this time, the Idaho
County Sheriff's Department dredged up a turn-of-the-century
anti-labor law to charge one group of protesters with "stealing
the road" by denying the loggers access to it.

Nothing like this had ever happened in Dixie, or the other
nearby town, Elk City, and the reaction was to ban Earth Firsters from these towns, announced by a big piece of spray-
painted plywood at the edge of town. It read, EARTH FIRST! KEEP
GOING. Posters showing a prototypical hippie with a target centered on his head were hung in businesses like the Dixie General Store. Activists were not allowed to buy gas or even use
the phone in Dixie, which was the only public telephone in a
seventy-mile radius. Accessing the Dixie store or pay phone
now became a revered sport. In addition, Highland Construction, the company building the roads, filed a civil suit claiming
over a million dollars in damages.

Because of the widespread belief that Ramon and I were
busy recruiting innocent college students to come to Idaho to
break the law, the Idaho state legislature was considering a law
making it illegal to be an Earth Firster. It would now be a felony with a mandatory one-year prison sentence to advocate
the obstruction of any logging road in Idaho. It was called the
Earth First! Law by the Idaho media. Even singing about blocking a logging road would be illegal.

Despite all of this, the Idaho news media was not interested
in the story. It was simply too far away, and too polemical to be
of interest. Few outside of Idaho County were even aware we
were at war.

Meanwhile, back in San Francisco, while enjoying the good life amongst a friendlier crowd, I was starting to realize that I was not cut out to be a consultant. Living in the Mission district with my new girlfriend Kristin Nelson on a thousand dollars a month was certainly better than the fifty dollars a month I'd survived on in Missoula. But somehow I felt that here in California I was just another one of hundreds, even thousands of forest activists. In Idaho, I could be universally hated by a large percentage of the state's population.

That Christmas, Ramon came for a visit to San Francisco.

He had some good news and some bad news. No one had bothered to show up for their court appearance in the civil suit, so twelve named activists and an additional two hundred Jane and John Does were now in default for a million-plus-dollar judgment against them. Activists were facing felony charges for road theft. One faced felony assault on an officer and jumped bail. And there was another activist in jail for a half year because he would not give his name.

In addition, the Forest Service issued a closure order where the logging was taking place to bar any protesters from being in the area. There was no money in the bank accounts. Worst of all, according to Ramon, there was, "No ink!" meaning negligible press coverage.

I listened to Ramon with sympathy. My heart went out to him. I'd been in his position before. However, I had no intention of leaving San Francisco and my new girlfriend. I also had no idea that while I was in the kitchen making spring rolls, Ramon was plying Kristin with martinis and tales of the wilds of Idaho. Walking from the kitchen into our tiny living room wiping my hands on my apron, I was greeted by Kristin.

"We are going to Idaho!" she squealed.

"Really," I responded. "When?"

"I want you to open an office in Moscow and to coordinate our legal defense," said Ramon matter-of-factly, as if the deal were already made. So Kristin and I packed our bags and left behind the beautiful city of San Francisco for the hostile wilds of Idaho.

Moscow was not a hostile place. Here the timber industry had less sway, and the biggest industry was Idaho State University. After a year in Dixie, Ramon had compared it to Paris during the war. Of course, he was neither in Paris during the war nor even in the military. But he was right. In Moscow we had local support, plenty of eager volunteers to staff the office, and the great martini bar in the Moscow Hotel.

We didn't actually have an office. Ramon was working out of the Royal Motel. Kristin discovered, to her chagrin, that our quarters consisted of a small moldy apartment in an old World War II–era military housing unit on the edge of Moscow. Aside from ourselves, it housed a half dozen other itinerant activists, Sarah Seeds from Seeds of Peace, a few pets, several boxes of rotting food scavenged from a Dumpster, and no furniture.

I was just trying to get oriented, when Earth Firsters from around the country converged on Moscow for a big meeting in January. Present were activists from Oregon, California, Montana, and some from as far away as Maine and Florida. The meeting was long, contentious, and inconclusive. At the core of the debate was a management issue. West Coast Earth First! asserted that Cove/Mallard was an Earth First! campaign. Therefore, all aspects of the campaign were the responsibility of the Earth First! leadership.

The problem was that by this time the activists in the trenches of the Cove/Mallard war had become a uniquely Idaho team, supported by Wild Rockies Earth First! The northern Rockies team bristled at any thought of being told what to do by people from Eugene or Berkeley. The West Coast activists simply could not fathom what we had been through, or what we were facing. This was not Redwood Summer. We were operating in some of the most remote country in the Lower 48 states, surrounded by hostile forces.

The ensuing leadership battle turned into a big fight.

During all of this, I was thinking about packing my bags for San Francisco when Missoulian Jake Kreilick approached me. With him was Ramon and a tall, lanky man with a beard and ponytail. He was Peter MacAusland, a house painter from Burlington, Vermont. He wanted to take us out to dinner and have a talk. Since Moscow was too small for such a meeting to go unnoticed by the dozens of Earth Firsters in town, we went to a dumpy Chinese restaurant across the river in Pullman, Washington.

I was in tears.

"These knuckleheads have no idea what's going on, and they want to tell us what to do, then go back to Berkeley, Eugene, or Garberville to smoke weed!" I ranted.

Peter was perplexed. "What can we do?" he asked.

I did have one idea. "We have to cut our tether to Earth First! How about we start a new group, call it the Cove/Mallard Coalition, and really start to mainstream this campaign," I said. "We need to start talking their language. Right now, no one in Idaho will work with Earth First!, and that includes me!"

Peter was quiet. We drank a few Tsing Tsaos, and finally he spoke.

"I haven't told anyone why I came out here," Peter said. "I've been reading about this struggle in the *Earth First! Journal*, and am really inspired. Last year my father died and left me a large amount of money in stocks as an inheritance. I don't need it or want it. So I'm cashing them in and was thinking of making a donation to Earth First! Obviously I'm now reconsidering that, but I think I can help you guys out."

Peter pledged twenty thousand dollars on the spot to launch the new organization.

Now, with an office in downtown Moscow, money in the bank, and some new volunteers, we got to work. The first order of business was to get the default judgments set aside. For this purpose, I hired a local attorney and we prepared for court. Before long, a legal team of considerable talent, most of them working pro bono, was assembled to tackle our mounting legal problems, including the list of felonies. We also maintained the camp, located on Ramon's purchased property near Dixie. Finally, we had a camp that the Freddies could not raid without a warrant. We also had fresh reinforcements—activists from Seeds of Peace.

When the Forest Service first drafted the Cove/Mallard sale in 1990, the Wilderness Society remained silent, as did the rest of the environmental movement. In a backroom deal, Cove/Mallard was traded off by so-called conservationists in exchange for the Forest Service allegedly protecting the nearby Meadow Creek roadless area. The election of Bill Clinton and environmental champion Al Gore had created hope for change in Washington, D.C. There was none.

In fact, the Democrats needed the popular vote of the timber states and did not want to appear hostile to such an important industry that employed so many people. The big conservation groups like the Sierra Club had less influence under the Clinton administration than they did under the twelve previous years of Republican rule.

Clinton wanted to solve the issue once and for all. In April of 1993, he assembled a grand summit in Portland and then crafted a secret compromise that would allow logging in road-less areas under the guise of fire prevention. Trees now had to be cut so they would not burn. It was attached to a spending bill and never debated. The so-called Salvage Rider did what no Republican could ever have gotten away with. It allowed commercial logging in federally protected roadless areas. Soon, millions of acres of the finest old-growth forests were on the chopping block, and logging accelerated again on the National Forest.

The Earth First! Law made its way through the legislature and was signed into law by Democratic Idaho Governor Cecil Andrus in 1993. We instantly began plotting how to break both the letter and spirit of the unconstitutional law.

The good news was that the courts had responded to Ron Mitchell and the Idaho Sporting Congress lawsuit. In February 1994, U.S. District Judge Harold Ryan ceased all road building and timber sales in Cove/Mallard until the Forest Service could prove that it wasn't in violation of the National Environmental Protection Act and the Endangered Species Act.

This was, as everyone knew, only a temporary reprieve. Since Earth First! had worked with the Idaho Sporting Congress, the moratorium was seen as a victory for the radical extremists. Our "victory" ensured a political backlash. It was important to use this valuable time to put the campaign on more solid footing and prepare for the eventual sellout that we all knew was coming.

Although logging was temporarily halted, we still needed

to maintain a physical presence in the timber-sale unit. We planted a garden, held nature hikes, and did biological surveys to document the presence of endangered or threatened species. We also launched several road shows to campuses across the country to flagrantly violate the Earth First! Law. We wrote articles for environmental newspapers, letters to the editor, went to Rotary Clubs and churches, and looked for any opportunity to get ready for the inevitable—the day the injunction was lifted.

I appeared on the steps of the Idaho capitol building on the Fourth of July wearing a suit with an American flag tie. I gave away small plastic shovels and implored citizens to dig up the illegal Jack Creek road. No matter how much we advocated stopping the road, no one would arrest us.

Summer ended. The snows came. Kristin and I decided to hunker down in Missoula and start the Ruckus Society, yet another environmental organization.

In December of 1994, the injunction was lifted and the trucks and bulldozers drove out to the Noble Road to begin a winter logging operation.

I received a phone call from Tom Fullum, an Earth Firster in Missoula.

"Are you going to break the law, Mike?" Tom asked.

"You know exactly what I'm thinking," I replied.

"We'll, I'm going with you," he declared.

We drove up to Cove/Mallard in his station wagon. On two pizza boxes, we had hastily scrawled a couple of slogans with Magic Markers. One read, SAVE COVE/MALLARD, the other stated, STOP ILLEGAL LOGGING. We met tactical chief Mike Bowersox and Seeds of Peace, Ramon and the Bus Brigade, and several others at the gate.

It was below zero on the Noble Road, and the snows were five feet deep. Seeds of Peace had dug several snow caves and a network of connecting trenches, all surrounding a large sunken fire pit. Ramon's bus was on the road serving coffee, hot chocolate, and old doughnuts scavenged from a Dumpster in Moscow. Spirits were high among the thirty or so protesters gathered at the gate to the Noble Road. This was the best opportunity to both break the Earth First! Law and to stop the logging, if only for a day or two.

The cops, the Freddies, and the loggers were gathering down the hill. We were outnumbered pretty good. We dug in. After a few very cold and tense moments, the trucks began to roll up the hill toward our position.

All thirty of us stood our ground on the ice-covered road. The string of vehicles was escorted by Idaho County Sheriff's Deputies, Forest Service Law Enforcement Officers (LEOs), and, of course, the media. The first truck hauled a large lowboy trailer carrying a D-9 bulldozer. It approached the gate to the Noble Road. The driver stopped, got out, didn't seem too upset, and began to put on his tire chains. The road had a steep grade that led down into the pristine canyon of the Main Salmon, considered a wilderness-river jewel.

The sheriff approached and announced that anyone who did not get off the road would be arrested, "For obstruction of a logging road, a felony punishable by a minimum one-year prison sentence upon conviction." As one, all the protesters moved to the side of the road with the exception of Tom and me. We stood silently as the cop read us our rights and placed us under arrest.

Then something strange happened. The cop who arrested me opened the door of his pickup truck and told me to get in, without handcuffing me. That had never happened before, and probably violated police protocols for safety. But there I was, riding up front. We began to talk on the long drive down to the Idaho County Jail in Grangeville. He gave me coffee from his thermos and some banana bread his wife had baked.

"Mike, we used to think you people were two-headed monsters," he offered. "But you guys have been up here for a while now. I used to think you were all crazy. But I'm not so sure you're the crazy ones anymore."

The next morning, Tom and I were in all the newspapers and on television. Finally, the Cove/Mallard timber sale was getting the attention it deserved. By the end of 1995, Cove/Mallard would be listed as Idaho's number-one local news story of the year.

Down in the Grangeville jail, Tom and I were booked and jailed for the night. In the morning, we were taken to the courthouse and introduced to the Idaho County prosecutor, Jeff Payne. We sat down at opposite tables, facing Idaho Magistrate Michael Griffin.

After the prosecutor presented the evidence, I asked for copies of the police report, knowing that the cops scarcely had the time to file them. I received the first of many continuances. Later in February, the judge, getting more and more irritated, pleaded with Tom and me to let the three prosecution witnesses enter testimony, since they had taken a second day off work for court. He said he would rule on our motion for a continuance afterwards. We agreed, conceding nothing, and the judge was visibly relieved.

The first witness was a Forest Service silviculturalist who had planned the sale. She was a young, enthusiastic forester, eager to get the cut out, and tried to explain the process that had produced the largest deficit timber sale in the history of the agency, and how she had followed all the rules. Tom Fullum, who had spent many years studying the timber sale, grilled her relentlessly. She finally admitted that she really didn't have a clear enough grasp of the myriad laws and regulations to state authoritatively that this timber sale was indeed legal, a prerequisite for conviction under the new law.

Next up was our arresting officer. He offered that we were polite, and with the exception of blocking the road for three hours, were very orderly. He even offered that Tom and I had persuaded the other protesters to get off the road while we stood our ground.

Finally, the truck driver took the stand. "Did you know that the protesters were at the gate?" asked the prosecutor.

"Yeah, they'd been up there for weeks," he responded.

"Were you worried about them?" the prosecution asked.

"Naw, not really, we've been up there for a while with no trouble."

"What did you do?"

"Well," he said. "I had to put my chains on anyway, so it was no big deal."

"What did you do after putting your chains on?" Payne inquired.

"By that time the protest was over, so I just took my truck down the road to unload the dozer to plow the road."

After this last witness finished his testimony, Judge Griffin had made a decision. He dismissed the charges. It did not even matter that we had not entered a motion to dismiss the case on constitutional grounds. Originally, we were to be represented by Idaho ACLU attorneys. But, under pressure from the Democrats in Boise, the ACLU backed off at the last minute, leaving Tom and me to represent ourselves in a felony case.

In the courtroom, we decided against filing any motions other than for a continuance. That way we could reserve our right to bump the judge if he seemed disposed against us. Judge Griffin dismissed the charges on lack of evidence of a crime. He stated two reasons for the dismissal: First, according to the truck driver, nothing had been impeded. Second, he noted that the prosecutor had failed to show that Tom and I had actually conspired with each other.

"True, they were both there with the same intentions," Griffin said. "But the evidence shows only that they conspired to keep the other protesters off the road once a warning was issued by law enforcement."

The prosecutor reserved his right to refile the charges. But the Earth First! Law, having failed its first test to hold accountable the very people it had targeted, had essentially been neutered. It remained on the books, but was never used again. Even when the protesters engaged in extended tree-sits, or when they dug up the road and rolled the heavy culverts down hillsides, or buried themselves in the road.

From this time on, most people arrested in Cove/Mallard would be charged with simple trespass, cited, and released. With the Earth First! Law no longer inhibiting our ability to block the road, the actions continued at a more robust level. Legally, we turned our attention to the other threat to our right to stop this road, the civil suit filed by Highland Construction in 1992 against the activists arrested that year.

The civil lawsuit was now our biggest legal hurdle in continuing the campaign. Because of the situation—in which

anyone who participated in a demonstration, whether blocking or obstructing any work or not, could be liable for a large
punitive damage award—it was getting hard to draw people to
come up to the protests.

If we wanted to succeed, we needed to escalate, and since
we were unwilling to damage their property, that meant organizing even larger demonstrations.

The summer of 1996 lived up to most of our expectations.
The campaign became bigger and more confrontational. Blockades and demonstrations became more frequent. Arrests were
now over one hundred, and we were able to maintain a full-
time presence on the road. In July, the annual Earth First!
Rendezvous was held in Cove/Mallard. Afterwards, an eighty-
six-day blockade on the Noble Road began to cause a tense
standoff. By summer's end, Cove/Mallard would be the most
controversial timber sale in the country.

That October we went back to the courts to fight the civil
suit. By this time we had twelve lawyers on staff, including a
constitutional law professor from the University of Idaho. On
October 30, 1996, twelve Cove/Mallard activists were saddled
with a $1.15 million judgment from the jury in the *Highland
Enterprises v. Earth First!* lawsuit. It came after a two-week trial
in a Grangeville kangaroo court. Many of the jurors were either working in the timber industry or were closely related to a
timber worker. This included a bartender in a logger bar in Elk
City who was married to a log-truck driver.

Highland was allowed by the judge to introduce evidence
of wide-scale property damage, even though those who were
arrested and named in the complaint did nothing more than
sit in front of the gate at the Jack Creek road. Much of the evidence used against us was gleaned from articles printed in

various Earth First! newspapers and written by people who had never been to Cove/Mallard.

It took the jury less than an hour to find the activists guilty, and that included time for their bathroom break. We were out $1.15 million, but hey, Ramon, we got ink! Besides, nobody had any money to pay up anyway. We were Lowbaggers.

In a story printed in the *New York Times*, Don Blewett, owner of Highland Enterprises, said he expected to see some payment over time because the jury's award would remain in effect for the defendants' lifetimes.

"If their Great-Aunt Matilda buys a Volkswagen van and she dies and gives it to one of them, that baby's mine," Mr. Blewett said. However, their greatest disappointment had come just before the trial started, when Ramon informed the judge that he had just filed for bankruptcy. This would mean that Highland could not go after the land in Dixie where we had our camp, one of the principal reasons for filing the lawsuit.

Another setback for Highland was that they were not allowed to collect their legal fees, which by this time had grown to almost a million dollars. Ramon responded to Blewett's threat to confiscate our property in a letter to the *Lewiston Journal* urging Blewett to go farther. "Don, don't stop when you get the [Ancient Forest Bus Brigade] bus. Quit your job, go drive around the country, and try to do something with your life other than destroying the last of the wilderness."

But the loss of the civil suit, the arrest of more than 150 activists—with some, like Jake Kreilick, serving long jail terms—or the raids by both law enforcement and timber industry goons could not deter the protesters. Neither could the violent assaults by loggers or the negative news coverage. Things were clearly beginning to change.

In the spring of 1997, when logging started again, so did the blockades. By now, the blockades included digging up the roads, and long tree-sits in the path of the coming road. In fall, the actions spread to the cities, including Region One head-quarters in Missoula, where activists chained themselves to the front doors and held vigils for weeks, suspended from tripods erected over the sidewalk. A new campaign to stop logging in Otter Wing, a timber sale near the Gospel Hump Wilderness, was launched by Seeds of Peace.

The fight struggled on, and in early 1999, even before Bill Clinton's moratorium on intrusions into roadless areas ended the entire debate, the logging and road-building ended. The battle in Cove/Mallard ended when Bruce Bernhardt became forest supervisor. Bernhardt announced that the remaining six unsold timber sales planned for Cove/Mallard would not be sold. According to Bernhardt, the forest had other priorities.

"[Cove/Mallard] is an intact ecosystem and in terms of eco-system restoration there are so many other places that need to be restored," he said in a story that appeared in the *Lewiston Morning Tribune*. Bernhardt made his announcement to halt cutting in Cove/Mallard even before President Clinton un-veiled his plan to permanently protect roadless areas, which included Cove/Mallard.

The timber industry was outraged, but there was little they could do. Their time had simply come and gone. A small bunch of hippie activists led by a retired insurance salesman had beaten them. What was supposed to have been a five-year project was shut down in the seventh year, with only a fraction of the job done. Both sides of the fight had taken a beating, but the timber industry ultimately lost.

A decade earlier, we had been labeled terrorists and anar-

chists for advocating and acting on a belief that would become
presidential mandate: that no intrusion into a roadless area
would be tolerated. In forest issues, you can't wait for the inter-
section of politics and science if you intend to save some trees.
Nobody wanted to admit that the Earth First! platform had
actually been right on since its inception twenty years earlier.

Forest Service officials said there were many factors that
motivated the decision to stop cutting in Cove/Mallard. The
listings of the bull trout, steelhead, and chinook under the Endangered Species Act helped. A nationwide $8.4 billion road-
maintenance backlog curbed the fiscal feasibility of building
new roads.

Ihor Mereszczak, a staff officer on the Nez Perce who had
been one of the projects' earlier supporters, was quoted in the
same article in the *Lewiston Morning Tribune.*

"We've realized we have a lot of road we need to manage, so
in the foreseeable future, it's hard to visualize we're going to
build any more roads," Mereszczak said. "If we can't manage
our roads, we can't maintain the environment. It's a holistic
process."

Was this really the same foe we had squared off against
originally?

Then Forest Service Chief Mike Dombeck's assistant, Chris
Wood, told the paper that the agency had a new outlook on
roads.

"I think the values and public sentiment have shifted, and
frankly, the sentiment of the Forest Service shifted from the
days of the big road projects in roadless areas," says Wood.

So the campaign did not end with a bang but with a whim-
per.

But the fact was that had the Cove/Mallard campaign not

been waged, the heart of the biggest roadless area outside of Alaska would have been cut out, and the case would have been moot. The scope and breadth of this resistance can hardly be overstated, especially when combined with the legal challenges. We have seen how these two tactics often work in unison. It creates a tremendous burden on the agency. Most of their resources are used responding to lawsuits, public criticism, and direct-action obstruction in the forest.

This was not the end of the timber wars, just another reprieve, as we prepared to meet the attacks of the coming Bush administration.

The lessons of Cove/Mallard are opposite of what one might think. Traditional grassroots conservation organizing models held that you needed local support, favorable media, and friendly relationships with the government agencies charged with protecting the public domain.

Yet in Idaho County conservationists had none of that. We weren't even allowed into local stores or restaurants. Media coverage, with the exception of the alternative press, was universally negative. No foundation would give us funding. No self-respecting environmental group would join our coalition. Yet through tenacity, audacity, and a strong belief that, win or lose, we were all doing the right thing, we outlasted them.

While this multi-year battle waged, the world around us changed. We were no longer unusual or even radical. The public now supported the "radical" positions of Earth First! They were against development in publicly owned roadless areas, against the logging of old-growth forests, and supported the protection of endangered species. The gray wolf had even been reintroduced into central Idaho, and now roamed in Cove/Mallard.

The Cove/Mallard Coalition lives on today as the Friends of the Clearwater, named after the river that drains much of the area. Gary Macfarlane, the director there for over a decade, is still monitoring Forest Service policies in central Idaho. Idaho now has a robust environmental movement, and a bull pen of competent environmental lawyers.

Most important, the chain saws and bulldozers have been silenced in Cove/Mallard, and you can once again hear the howl of a wolf float through the stillness of the night.

9

Greenpeace Confronts the Mahogany Pirates

With a snow-white beard and hair, Marco Kaltofen looks older than his thirty-eight years. Energetic, almost manic, this morning Marco is in no real hurry. He is driving in the rental truck in front of me as we careen down Pico Boulevard in sunny downtown Santa Monica. It's 1986. We are going to a birthday party. We are each joined by two other people in the cabs of our vehicles. We are all wearing haz-mat suits, complete with respirators. Both of the flatbed trucks are filled with black fifty-five-gallon drums containing toxic waste we had daringly raided from the famous Stringfellow Acid Pits the night before. Each drum has a white skull and crossbones stenciled on it. When we arrive, the Occidental Oil party is well under way.

We approach the Santa Monica Civic Auditorium, and just as we had suspected, the security guards and police are out in force. Marco had introduced himself to Occidental security the morning before, and I had given him my card with the title Greenpeace Chief of Security, in case he needed to reach us for any reason. Marco informed them that we would be delivering a birthday present for Armand Hammer, the CEO of Occidental, for this occasion, which coincided with Oxy's annual stockholders meeting. Not knowing what else to say, the cops just warned us, "We will be waiting for you."

And they were. We spotted them just as we turned left at the corner of Main Street. At the entrance to the parking lot, there were several cops, security guards, and Oxy company men, all wearing suits and uniforms, holding radios, and waiting. They saw us and started talking on their radios. More cops rushed toward the steel gate of the large parking lot in front of the auditorium, which was closed. Still more cops were gathered at the entrance to the building. They watched as we approached.

The parking lot is separated from the main building by a large lawn, which continues to the street and runs alongside the main concert hall. Besides a few palm trees, a few park benches, and a utility pole, there is nothing between us and the entrance. Up ahead on the right is the driveway with the gate and the cops, but Marco veers sharply right, jumps the curb between the palm tree and a park bench, and proceeds to crush a KEEP OFF THE GRASS sign. I have no choice but to follow.

The cops knew they'd been had. Environmentalists didn't drive on the grass. Yet here we were, barreling across the lawn, closing in on the bank of glass doors that formed the only entrance to the auditorium.

Rallying, they rushed toward Marco's truck and managed to get in front. Marco didn't stop. He dropped the transmission into neutral and gunned the engine. As Marco's truck pushed forward, the cops moved, walking backwards. Yelling and gesturing with their hands, they continued in this fruitless effort until we had driven under the chevron-shaped front canopy and parked the trucks a few feet from a long bank of glass doors. Soon we were surrounded.

Quickly, without paying the cops any attention, we dismounted from the cabs of the trucks. Our job now was to unload the drums and set up police tape around the scene. This would prove impossible and unnecessary. A cop gently touched Marco and he fell to the ground. We all quickly joined him and sat together in front of the lead truck. We were all duly arrested. Action over!

But it wasn't over. The rental trucks had a safety feature that would set the emergency brakes if you removed the key from the ignition. The keys had mysteriously disappeared. The tow truck couldn't budge the rigs. We had rented the vehicles on the other side of Los Angeles, and now calls were going out for spare keys.

"What's in those drums?" the head cop asked.

"Just some leachate from the Stringfellow Acid Pits," Marco responded earnestly. "It's a birthday present for Mr. Hammer, and I believe it belongs to him. We are just returning it to its rightful owner."

A Los Angeles County haz-mat team was called in, wearing identical Tyvek suits, and dutifully took our place at the action. We were carted off to the Santa Monica Jail. The haz-mat crew remained at the auditorium for the remainder of the meeting. The leachate in the barrels was not toxic. Leachate in this case refers to rainwater from the surrounding hills that had been diverted away from the pits into a steel tank.

Oxy had scheduled a big press conference for that day, announcing the acquisition of Hooker Chemical, the company responsible for Love Canal. Mr. Hammer disappeared quickly out the back door of the auditorium to dodge the media, which were now asking him all the wrong questions versus the softballs he had expected. He did not get any cake and ice cream. The story would appear on the front page of the business section of the *Los Angeles Times*. So would the photo of us with the toxic waste.

This was my first action with Greenpeace, but it would not be my last. For the next twenty years, I would be working with the "firm" on various projects around the world. During that time, I watched Greenpeace grow from a small organization with a lot of members and money into a much larger organization with over a thousand employees. Then, in 1990, I watched the U.S. office shrink as it lost staff, members, and money. Today it is still a large organization with considerable resources at its disposal, but one that has undergone tremendous change.

With its sailing ships and daring feats on the high seas, Greenpeace has become the largest, best known, and most successful conservation group on Earth. Starting with the 1972 voyage of the *Phyllis Cormack* to stop a nuclear bomb test in Amchitka, Alaska, the Greenpeace story is perhaps the most exciting and heroic of all stories in the history of the modern-day conservation movement. It can also be a difficult story to understand. Facts, myths, and symbols are viewed from many angles by all the individuals who were involved. Even its founders disagree over key elements of the story, and much of it remains undocumented.

Greenpeace's media strategies and campaigns are taught in mass communication classes. Greenpeace forever changed the communications field with their skillful use of dramatic footage from daring actions in exotic locations. Greenpeace was also a pioneer in the field of fund-raising and membership development. The organization transformed a small office in Vancouver into an international network of thirty separate but aligned offices spanning the globe. All of this resulted in a political pressure group with enormous power to move public opinion and force both governments and the largest multinational corporations to take action.

I was hired by Greenpeace USA's first executive director Richard Grossman in the fall of 1986 with the dubious title of Direct Action Team Coordinator. Grossman thought my experience with Earth First! might be useful in bringing some new ideas and energy into the group. The group had just suffered the sinking of its flagship, the *Rainbow Warrior*, resulting in the loss of a crew member in the explosion. My background was in forest conservation, and in 1986, Greenpeace was just becoming engaged in that issue.

In 1984, at one of their international meetings, when faced with a choice to campaign for protection of the Amazon rain forest or Antarctica, Greenpeace chose Antarctica. This was due mostly to the fact that they could use their ships and maritime experience to operate in the remote seas, and their ability to lobby governments to pass and enforce international treaties and conventions. It was also, according to one witness, due to the influence of a chief fund-raiser. When asked to weigh in on the decision, he responded, "There's a lot of money in them penguins."

And so there was. Greenpeace became the first nongovernmental organization to set up and supply a permanent base on the shores of Antarctica. With the help of Greenpeace and other organizations, the southern ocean around Antarctica was formally designated a whale sanctuary in 1994 by the International Whaling Commission (IWC), making the region permanently off-limits to commercial whaling. Greenpeace was able to help create an Antarctic Whaling Sanctuary, regulate international commercial fishing fleets, and get an international agreement against militarizing Antarctica.

Events in Canada, however, would intervene. In 1992, I met David Peerla, from Greenpeace Canada, at a meeting for the new Greenpeace Forest Team. Peerla's chief concern was the toxic chemicals used and discarded into the environment by the pulp-and-paper industry. He had been trying to build an alliance with the unions that represented the paper mills. He was using what he called a "market campaign" to pressure Canadian paper companies to discontinue the use of chlorine to bleach the wood pulp. Chlorine used in this manner produces prodigious amounts of toxic waste that gets dumped in the air, the water, and in landfills. Since he knew that the chances of government or industry reforms in Canada were unlikely any time soon, his strategy was to convince the large European customers, such as publishers of books and magazines, to cancel their contracts with Canadian pulp corporations under threat of a secondary boycott.

Like most Canadians of his day, he saw nothing wrong with old-growth logging, and realized that if no old-growth trees were logged, there wouldn't be much of a timber industry left in British Columbia. But, the timber industry was taking care of that itself. In fifty years, most of Canada's ancient forests had been felled. The mill workers simply were not going to listen to any group opposed to old-growth logging.

There were, however, a few small groups who *were* opposed to the logging. The Friends of Clayoquot Sound, The Western

Canada Wilderness Coalition, and a number of first nations like the Nuxalk and Haida were also opposed. Actions of non-violent civil disobedience were common on the coast of British Columbia, even in the years before Earth First! began to use them in Oregon. The activists in British Columbia were a diverse lot, but a large component was young, white, and lived alternative lifestyles. While they lived in logging country, few were involved in the timber industry. Many sported long hair, beards, and dressed in a manner that set them apart from the locals. The timber war here, as elsewhere, was a clash of cultures.

Greenpeace Canada forbade me to meddle in the Canadian forests issues in 1990. That same year, Greenpeace USA had sent me up to Alaska to assist the local conservationists in stopping the logging of old-growth forests on the Tongass National Forest. The Alaskans were unanimously opposed to any more logging of their ancient forests, or any new roads in the remaining roadless areas. This was no longer a radical position to hold in Alaska, as the largest trees were not being used for the high-value lumber they could provide. Alaska spruce, for example, is valued for the making of fine pianos and other wooden musical instruments. These eight-hundred-year-old spruce trees were ground into pulp and exported to Japan to manufacture cellophane. The mill waste was dumped into the ocean, fouling the water and killing fish, or burned in incinerators, where toxic chemicals entered the air and settled into the soil, stunting tree growth for miles downwind.

A moratorium on logging ancient forests in Alaska by Greenpeace would not go unnoticed in Canada. David Peerla was concerned that a call for the outright ban on old-growth logging on the Tongass would end up alienating the union and mill workers in British Columbia, to say nothing of the rest of the country. This could jeopardize his efforts to get the pulp-and-paper industry to stop using chlorine in the manufacturing process and adopt newer technology that used oxygen for the same results.

Officially, Greenpeace was in favor of sustainable old-growth logging, even though the scientific studies suggested that any logging in ancient forest was unsustainable, and that temperate coastal rain forests like the ones in southeast Alaska and British Columbia were the most endangered forest ecosystems on the planet. Unlike Canada, Greenpeace USA and most large American environmental groups had by now agreed on the need to save the remaining ancient forests. When I informed Peerla of this, he called me an imperialist. "Greenpeace will never sit in the middle of a muddy logging road like those hippies," he warned me.

In Alaska, we blockaded the loading dock at Alaska Pulp Company's Sitka mill for a day, visited many of the coastal communities, including Native Alaskan villages and towns, and staged a protest against the logging in the Tongass at the Governor's Mansion in Juneau. Afterwards, we had planned to sail down through British Columbia from Alaska on the *Rainbow Warrior*. Peerla had prohibited me from conducting any anti-timber activity in Canada, even though we would be sailing by the Great Bear Rain Forest, one of the largest unprotected coastal rain forests on Earth. I had no choice but to comply.

We did make one stop in Canada, at the town of Haida on Queen Charlotte Island. There, we were met by Mike Nicols, the mayor of Haida, who took the crew of the *Rainbow Warrior* deep into the forest to witness a rare performance of the Haida pit dance for nonnatives. The Haida had successfully fought logging on the southern part of Queen Charlotte Island, which they called Haida Gwaii. They were now engaged in an effort to kick MacMillan-Bloedel, which was Canada's largest timber company at the time, off the rest of their island. Sitting on Mike Nicols's front porch, we watched the *Haida Princess*, the world's largest self-propelled log barge, cross over to the mainland twice a day with $2 million worth of Haida-owned old growth on board each trip.

But time would not stand still any longer for Greenpeace Canada. With the 1993 government decision to clear-cut 74 percent of Clayoquot Sound's ancient forest, anger over logging in British Columbia led to the largest act of modern civil resistance in Canadian history. It took nine hundred arrests before the destruction of BC's ancient forests was beamed into televisions around the world, and Greenpeace Canada and Greenpeace International were drawn into the conflict.

In 1993, David Peerla and much of the Greenpeace International leadership would be arrested on the muddy logging roads of Clayoquot Sound. Greenpeace was now opposed to all logging in old growth, a courageous moral position that caused them to lose both members and income in Canada. In order to prevent companies from sourcing their timber from other endangered forests, Greenpeace finally had to call for an end to logging in ancient forests worldwide. Finally, they adopted a forest policy in line with the World Rainforest Movement's Penang Declaration of 1989.

David Peerla had gotten religion, as had everyone else among the more than twelve thousand people who had participated in the Clayoquot Sound campaign. It was hard for anyone to witness this kind of destruction without getting angry, and now Peerla was looking for an angle or some new form of leverage that Greenpeace could use to increase the pressure on MacMillan-Bloedel. The resulting economic research would lead to Greenpeace, Rainforest Action Network, Natural Resource Defense Council, and the Sierra Club launching market campaigns against all British Columbian timber products. The boycotts were first aimed at Europe and the United States. But given Greenpeace's reach, the boycotts soon spread to Japan, Australia, New Zealand, and even China.

The market approach developed by Peerla was different from your traditional boycott, which usually entailed asking consumers to refuse to buy the companies' products—as RAN did with Burger King. This strategy works well if the company has a large retail presence, and especially if they have to buy a lot of advertising in order to maintain market share in a very competitive business like fast food restaurants. MacBlo did not sell directly to the consumer, but to other large users of pulp and timber, such as lumber yards, furniture stores, paper companies, and magazine and catalog companies. By threatening a secondary boycott, conservation groups were able to force the cancellation of large contracts with MacBlo, affecting their bottom line.

Hit them in the pocketbooks, and they'll change their ways. The campaign to protect the Great Bear Rain Forest succeeded when more than eighty companies, including Ikea, Home Depot, Staples, and IBM committed to stop selling wood and paper products made from ancient forests, called the Good Wood Agreement.

Now Greenpeace could turn their attention to the Amazon rain forest.

The first order of business was to open an office in the Amazon in the frontier town of Manaus, Brazil. Oddly, this had never been done. Most international groups who had any presence in Brazil had their offices in Rio de Janeiro, which is about as close to the Amazon as San Francisco is to Alaska. Greenpeace also assembled a crack staff of Brazilians, including many who lived and worked along the Amazon, led by Paulo Adario, a charismatic and dedicated man who had received many death threats in the course of his work.

Each year, Greenpeace sent a ship up the Amazon to enlist supporters among the locals and indigenous groups, and to document the illegal timber industry. Their goal was to end illegal logging, as most mahogany is cut on native lands without permission or compensation, as required by Brazilian law. The majority of Amazon logging violates government controls. Illegal mahogany opens the door for illegal logging of other species, and for widespread exploitation of the Brazilian Amazon by miners, farmers, and ranchers who travel looking for cheap undeveloped land. No reliable legal chain of custody exists for mahogany, documents are commonly forged, and the key players in its trade, known as the Mahogany Kings, were ruthless with contacts in the highest level of government.

Mahogany is usually cut during the dry season. When the rains return and the water levels rise, the logs are floated down the creeks, tributaries, and adjoining rivers and cabled together into giant rafts. Then the mahogany is towed down the river by tugboats, and in those days, right past the Greenpeace office in Manaus. With few logging roads in the Amazon, most timber is transported this way. The advantage for Greenpeace was that they could now monitor the timber heading to Belem, at the mouth of the Amazon. Once it hit the ocean, the wood was loaded on ships bound for ports in the United States, Europe, Japan, and China.

This illegal trade was an open secret in Brazil, and Greenpeace now launched an aggressive plan to interdict these shipments in as many different countries as possible. This they did by boarding ships in foreign ports and chaining themselves to the cargo, or by blockading the ports and preventing the timber from being loaded. Because Greenpeace had thirty offices all over the world, these actions caused a very embarrassing situation for the Brazilian government, which had tried to portray itself as a careful steward of the Amazon rain forest, an iconic world treasure. In response to a loss of face, the Brazilian government began to crack down on the illegal logging in the Amazon in order to protect what little legal logging remained in the rest of the country. The fear of an international boycott of all Brazilian timber was a powerful motivator. The hard lessons of the Great Bear Rain Forest campaign were not lost on Brazil.

In 2001, I was again hired by the Greenpeace forest campaign. My assignment was to locate and board a ship transporting illegal mahogany into the United States during the meeting of CITES, the Convention on the Illegal Trade in Endangered Species, an international body set up to end the trade in endangered wildlife. Proposals that mahogany should be declared an endangered species were to be presented at this meeting, the first tree species ever to be added to the list. Such a declaration would make it illegal to import mahogany by any country, and would go a long way toward ending the trade.

When first offered the job, I certainly had no wish to move back to Washington, D.C., and sit in a cubicle every day. I called Steve Shallhorn, the new campaign coordinator, and left him a message informing him of my decision. Shallhorn was from the Canadian office, a legend in the firm for coordinating some huge campaigns. Later that day, he called me and invited me out to a local bar on Dupont Circle called the Big Hunt. An old chum from the London office, Mike Harold, would be there. He was the one who first offered me the job.

When I entered the bar, I found the duo sitting in front of two pints of beer. Talk was very cordial. They discussed the big campaign plan. I listened with interest. After a few more pints, I began to explain why I wouldn't take the assignment. They looked surprised, and at that moment I realized that Shallhorn had not gotten my phone message. There was an uncomfortable silence, and then the two continued the conversation amongst themselves in very excited tones, as if I wasn't there. I began to feel invisible. It became clear to me that if I refused this assignment, I would be missing out on something big. Another pint, and my mind changed.

"Okay," I promised, "I'll get you a ship."

We ordered another round, and I was let in on the plan.

"We are going to hit as many illegal timber ships in as many different places in the world as we can. The thing is that we're all going to do it at the same time," said Shallhorn.

Mike Harold interjected, "We need at least one action in the U.S. This is the largest market and a very important one in terms of media coverage. We've gotta step up the pressure on importing countries and at the same time pressure the exporting countries who are logging illegally under their laws."

I woke up the next morning with a headache—and an obligation to seize a ship. When I got to the U Street Greenpeace office, the large maze of suites was almost entirely deserted, with coffee mugs filled with mold sitting on cluttered desks. There were half-eaten lunches undisturbed in front of dusty computer screens. I had seen this before. There had been a slaughter here. You could still see the blood and hair on the walls.

Mike Harold had been one of the victims of the long knives. I helped him pack up his furniture as he explained the situation to me. There had been a massive downsizing. The board was forced out, a new board installed, and the executive director had been canned. A search was on for a new one, the action team was on the West Coast with the *Arctic Sunrise*, the new Greenpeace ship. The *Arctic Sunrise* was trolling for high donors. I would be working for the international office and would be paid in English pounds. This helped to explain why I was offered the job. No one ever calls me unless they're desperate.

The chain-of-custody question proved to be a problem again. False documents for shipments of illegal timber, which were difficult to define as such in the first place, were accepted without question by customs in ports across the United States. It was impossible to prove that anybody knew the timber was illegal.

Fortunately, there was one person left in the U Street Greenpeace office who knew how to find out. Scott Paul had just returned from an extended trip to Brazil, working with Paulo Adario documenting illegal logging on the Amazon River. We soon assembled a team including Twilly Cannon, Jim Ford, Carol Gregory, and eventually Adrienne Stauffer. For an action team, we assembled an assortment of former Greenpeacers, Rainforest Action Network volunteers, Earth Firsters, and a few Ruckus Society members. We also had six Greenpeacers from Europe and a few actual employees of the former regime that were still hanging around the U Street office, long ago dubbed "the House of Pain."

We found a bulk-timber carrier transporting raw logs stacked high on the decks from Belem. It was bound for Savannah, Georgia.

Our crew drove past the security gate in a white van with SAVANNAH REFRIGERATION AND HEATING on its side. Dexter, our driver, told the guard we were responding to an emergency breakdown of the compressor that ran the coolers. Wearing white coveralls and helmets, we caught the ship unloading. Four Europeans chained themselves to the hold while two more rappelled down the side of the ship and unfurled a banner that said STOP ILLEGAL LOGGING.

These two climbers quickly had their ropes cut by the angry longshoremen and were dropped into the Savannah River. Wearing heavy climbing gear, the protesters began to sink. Anticipating such a scenario, two Greenpeace Zodiac boats motored in to fish out the two climbers turned divers. One reporter would later call the waters "alligator infested." Although this boarding received scant U.S. media attention outside of Georgia, it was front-page news in Brazil, and part of an international boarding effort. More than a dozen ships were hit in as many days.

The Brazilian government responded by making it illegal to export mahogany without proof that it was legally harvested. They staged a few raids, accompanied by Paulo Adario and several members of the newly formed Forest Crimes Unit. These photos appeared all over the world, including in the United States. The mahogany trade was finally getting the attention it deserved, and political pressure was mounting for global reforms. But as long as countries like the United States turned a blind eye toward the mahogany that entered their ports, reforms in Brazil would be ineffective. The timber was worth a lot of money, and corruption was rife all the way up the supply chain.

The long-overdue reforms to the tropical timber trade would be discussed at the international Convention on Biological Diversity meeting at The Hague in 2002. Building on the success of the last "opera," as these coordinated international actions were called by code, Greenpeace wanted an even bigger production this time. By now I had a full-time job as the Forest Campaign Director and a desk in the new Greenpeace Chinatown office, complete with a new boss, board, staff, and a bunch of Europeans and Canadians who were intent on rebuilding the failing U.S. franchise.

At its peak in the mid-1980s, Greenpeace had more than 5 million supporters worldwide. By 1994, the numbers dropped to 4 million, and since have fallen to 2.4 million. The new management, under John Passacantando, working with the European team, cut costs and reorganized the campaigns to rebuild the campaign team. Greenpeace was again ready for action.

To crack the chain-of-command question, we would focus on the furniture industry—the biggest customers of mahogany. The furniture was very expensive—no company wanted to risk its reputation and profit by being connected to the destruction of the rain forests. In October, two members of the Forest Crimes Unit, Tim Keating and John Piccone, agreed to go on the road and check out every lead they could find. I gave them a rental car, a cell phone, a laptop, and a credit card. I told them not to return until they had documents, or until January 1, whichever came first. By then, my budget would be spent and it would be difficult to justify more time and expenses for further research. Then we would have to sit out the opera, bringing dishonor to our office in the eyes of our international allies.

At the time, Tim Keating was the foremost expert on the tropical timber trade in the United States. Piccone's ability to penetrate corporate security was legendary in both Greenpeace and the Rainforest Action Network. Eventually Keating and Piccone were combing through Dumpsters behind the offices of the major lumber distributors' yards.

One late night in December, I was lying in bed when the phone rang. I answered. It was Piccone's voice.

"It's the document fairy."

Sleepy, I was still confused.

"Tim and I are in a Dumpster with a flashlight, and some secretary has just dumped a year's worth of files in this Dumpster before going on Christmas vacation. We've got everything: manifests, invoices, even their line of credit with the mills in the upper Amazon."

There was a Santa Claus! I went back to bed. This was big, but we still had another big problem. Since 9/11, all the ports that received shipments from Belem were under Code Orange security alert. Not only did this mean more cops, but it also meant a more serious threat of criminal charges, maybe even being fired upon.

Scott Paul and Adrienne Stauffer combed through the mountain of documents Keating and Piccone had brought from North Carolina, and they prepared a detailed report on the movement of illegal timber from the Amazon to North Carolina. The reports were sent to all Greenpeace offices around the world for fact-checking, especially to the Brazilian office.

The Forest Crimes Unit had been working on a report on the mahogany trade, due for release in the fall. The documents were quickly added to it, along with a legal analysis detailing what laws were being broken and by whom. It was a damning document, and one that could not be ignored. Now the illegal timber trade was not just a matter of lax enforcement and corruption in Brazil. The importing countries, by knowingly buying from mills that exclusively launder timber from native lands, were actually creating the problem.

On September 26, 2001, Greenpeace released its report, naming seventy U.S. companies that had purchased illegal timber. A month later, all mahogany operations in Brazil were frozen. After an investigation, Operation Mahogany was launched, leading to dramatic raids by Greenpeace members and heavily armed Brazilian environmental enforcement. The Brazilian government used Greenpeace ships and planes. When the smoke cleared, $7 million of illegal mahogany was seized.

By April 2002, we were ready to strike in the United States. I went down to Miami with Greenpeace volunteer James Brady. The container ship *APL Jade* was headed for the Port of Miami, and we had learned the *Jade* had carried illegal mahogany in the past. Because of the nature of the sea-freight industry, containers of lumber could be unloaded and reloaded, and arrive at their destinations by various routes. It was a shell game, but there was a nut under each shell, because the *Jade* ran a regular route from Belem. It had carried some mahogany on each of its voyages over the last two years. I explained this to Andrea Durbin, and she gave us the go-ahead to seize the ship.

We rented a condo in South Beach near the port and kept watch on the ship traffic. With the Greenpeace action team once again deployed on the West Coast with the best equipment, I commandeered some old rubber boats from the Greenpeace warehouse, assembled a motley crew of the usual suspects, and went to work. The *APL Jade*, 965 feet long and weighing in at 53,519 tons, is one of the largest ships ever built. Only aircraft carriers and oil tankers are bigger. To enter the Port of Miami, the ship would have to call a pilot to steer it through the channel. By listening to the radio scanner, we would hear the call. The pilot boat would then leave from the Coast Guard base.

The trick to boarding a large ship is to position a Zodiac beneath a bridge at the entrance to the channel. When the pilot's radio call is intercepted, beat the pilot boat to the ship, and climb the ladder the crew would put down to receive the pilot. Once on deck, the boarding party would rush to the cranes, climb them, and chain themselves to the control cab, which would prevent any unloading. They also would deploy a banner that said PRESIDENT BUSH, STOP ILLEGAL LOGGING.

A problem developed right away. We were able to get Hillary Hosta and Scott Anderson, the two climbers, onto the pilot ladder as planned, but instead of climbing on deck, they were denied by a locked steel door. The activists were unable to reach the deck and deploy their banner. It was time for Plan B. Except, we didn't have one.

Improvising, Pele Pederson, a Swedish sailor with military experience, was in a rental boat ferrying media and observers and began to escort the ship through the channel flying a flag that said SAVE THE AMAZON. He was soon joined by a Coast Guard patrol boat and a Miami police boat, who signaled for him to stop. He did so dutifully.

When the two boats pulled alongside and prepared to board, Pele gunned the engines and took off in the opposite direction. The two boats lost time and distance, as they turned to give pursuit. The police boats were much larger and faster, and soon closed the gap. Once again, the cops pulled up alongside Pele's boat. Once again, Pele gunned the engines and speed off in another direction. This continued for some time. A crowd cheering Pele on formed along the channel.

I watched this from the deck of a local bar. I had a perfect view of the Coast Guard base, the gantry cranes where the *Jade* would be berthed, and the ship channel. In a pouch around my waist, I had several thousand dollars in cash, bail money for my crew, so I had to stay away from the action to avoid arrest. After a while, the ship had made it to its destination with our two climbers still on board. Pele finally surrendered to the authorities, who were feeling the sting of humiliation by being outrun by smaller craft in front of so many people. All were taken to jail.

The Coast Guard and the Miami police were ready to release the crew when the FBI arrived and filed federal charges for boarding an arriving vessel under an obscure law that prohibited "sailor mongering." The Greenpeace activists spent the weekend in jail.

Incredibly, U.S. authorities failed to seize the mahogany on the *Jade*. Instead, the ship proceeded from the Port of Miami to Charleston, where it unloaded seventy tons of mahogany.

As the summer drew on, Operation Mahogany continued seizing illegally harvested mahogany in Brazil. U.S. officials concluded that, without appropriate assurances from the Brazilian government, the United States could not accept shipments of mahogany. In late July, seven United States–based timber-product importers sued the U.S. government in District Court in Washington, D.C., for release of several shipments of mahogany held in U.S. custody. The U.S. government refused to release the mahogany. The District Court ruled that while the mahogany was indeed property of U.S. importers, the cargo could not enter the United States. It sat on the docks for months, in legal limbo.

This would turn out to be my last action for Greenpeace. I resigned my position and returned to Oregon to help fight logging in southern Oregon's Siskiyou National Forest. Illegal logging is not just an issue in the rain forests of the Amazon and Africa. It happens every day in America. In the Siskiyou, bowing to political pressure from the timber industry and the politicians they control, the United States Forest Service is ignoring its own rules and regulations, liquidating the old growth and selling timber below market value in order to keep the sawmills running in Roseburg.

There is a reason that environmental groups win most all their lawsuits. The timber companies are breaking the law. When laws are not followed, citizens have to demand enforcement. Environmentalists have to do the work of investigator, lawyer, and prosecutor. But the foxes are still guarding the henhouse. Until we treat the destruction of the ancient forests like the crime it is, we will continue to witness its disappearance. Most people I encounter abroad are surprised that we haven't protected our remaining ancient forests here in America.

The Greenpeace Forests Crimes Unit is an unprecedented international effort to enforce the law. But it shouldn't be up to underfunded environmental groups to make sure corporations and governments follow important environmental laws. Enforcing the law is the duty of sovereign governments. Greenpeace broke the law when it seized the mahogany ship, but this action was taken to intervene in the commission of a crime. Mahogany is safer now. But for many other species of tropical timber, no protection exists. Greenpeace still has more work to do before it can rest.

10

Raising a Ruckus Society

The Golden Gate Bridge came into view as I drove toward the water from San Francisco's relentless hills. It was just before dawn, November 1996. The day was unusually clear with low winds—perfect weather for hanging a massive banner on the iconic landmark. Soon I was on the bridge, driving north-bound in a rented van. In the lane next to me was Rasim Ba-bameto, doing the same thing. Rasim grabbed his radio to talk to Richard Dillman, who was in the Greenpeace communications van on one of the bridge's overlooks, surveying traffic and scanning police channels to provide us with intelligence.

"It's showtime," Dillman said, giving Rasim the green light on the action.

With that, we stopped our cars in the center of the bridge. At the exact same time, two cars in the southbound lane did the same thing. And just like that, all traffic came to a stand-still on one of the world's busiest bridges.

We swiftly unloaded from the vehicles. I was wearing Day-Glo orange and carrying a stop sign to wave at the cars behind us. Others set up plastic barricades. Within seconds, four climbers wrapped ropes around the large supporting cables on opposite sides of the roadway and attached their harnesses. Soon they were above the crowd of startled tourists. The cables resembled the trunks of large trees, and the climbers ascended ever higher, inching their ropes up the cable much like a logger would climb a tree. From up on the cables, actor Woody Harrelson motioned with his thumb that his side was ready. Woody had spent the last three days training with this team in a warehouse in Oakland, where a wooden mockup of the cables had been constructed.

"Set the curtain line," team leader John Sellers calmly barked into his radio. A thin rope was quickly laid across the four blocked lanes of the bridge. This line would be tied to a much stouter rope and used to pull a large banner across the Golden Gate on carabineers; much like a shower curtain is hung on a curtain rod. So far, everything was going smoothly, just as we had practiced it in the three days leading up to the event.

This assault on one of the most famous structures on earth was Woody's idea. He had been standing around the campfire with a group of Earth Firsters in southern Humboldt County when the talk turned to action. Realizing a job this big would call for some extra help, Woody and the Earth Firsters called on Greenpeace and the Rainforest Action Network.

I got the call and set out from Missoula, Montana, with Rasim and Twilly Cannon in a rented minivan for San Francisco, where Sellers, aka Goat, was busy drilling a team of more than fifty people in an effort to tackle the holy grail of protest targets, hanging a banner on the Golden Gate Bridge. Two previous attempts had been made in past years, and both had failed due to the vigilance of the bridge security. On our team, we had veterans from both these previous attempts. This time we would not fail.

Back on the bridge, the script deviated from plan. A very large bald man in surgeon's scrubs exited his car and began to confront the activists blocking traffic. He was angry and aggressive, and seeing the curtain line lying on the roadway, put his foot and accompanying three hundred pounds on it. With this act of defiance, he had effectively stopped the action. Within minutes, police would arrive, and without a curtain line to hang the banner on, this action would fail just as the others had. I could see Woody and Celia Alerio on the bridge cables, pulling hard on the rope, holding pressure on the curtain line, but unable to get it off the ground. The bald man was standing a few feet in front of me, facing the opposite direction. He stared down the protesters in front of him as if daring them to try to dislodge him.

Something had to be done, and done quickly. The bald man was too big to be moved without a shoving match, and this would create problems, especially if a fight broke out. He certainly looked ready for a fight, and we were nonviolent. Nevertheless, I decided I had to bump him off.

I walked briskly in the direction of the large man, but just a little to his left side, as if walking toward something else. He saw me out of the corner of his eye but didn't pay much attention, because I wasn't looking at him, or paying him any notice. I was just about to pass by him, when he turned his head from me. With that, I veered sharply to my right, bumped him, and disappeared into the growing crowd.

"What the fuck!" he hollered as he lost his balance and

stumbled off the curtain line. Celia and Woody were still pulling on the line. As soon as the man's weight was off the line, it
snapped up about twelve feet above the deck of the bridge.
Woody and Celia began attaching heavier rope that could support the banner to the line.

At this point, the large man was even more agitated, and
glaring at me, but I kept walking fast, not looking back at him.
I put enough distance between the two of us to avoid an alter-
cation. Two police officers, who happened to be in an unmarked vehicle a few cars behind the barricade, had by now
arrived on the scene and tried to assess the situation, but they
were too late—the curtain line was drawn tight above the
deck. Seeing that our work was done, we dismantled the barricades and piled back in the vehicles, leaving the climbers to
stretch their massive banner across the roadway. On the banner was a message from Woody to timber-tycoon Charles Hurwitz: HURWITZ, AREN'T REDWOODS MORE PRECIOUS THAN GOLD?
The rental vans zoomed off, leaving the police alone on the
bridge to admire our work.

With helicopters circling overhead, Woody was hosting
live interviews on his cell phone, and the Bay Area television
and radio stations were airing wall-to-wall coverage. By noon,
the point had been made, and the climbers came down after
rolling up their banner. They were arrested by the San Francisco Police Department. After posting bail, Woody flew out to
New York City for the talk-show circuit. While it would still be
more than a decade until the Headwaters Forest was fully
saved, this was one of the high-water marks of the struggle, a
day when everyone in the country would hear about the plight
of the last redwoods. In the process, Charles Hurwitz became
environmental enemy number one to millions of Americans.

It also gave birth to a new front in the environmental movement. The team that John Sellers assembled for the Golden Gate action was the core of a new environmental organization that would push the limits of political activism in the era of modern media. Gathering a diverse group of seasoned activists from the most confrontational environmental groups in the world, the group would eventually be named the Ruckus Society, and would dedicate itself to training a new generation of environmental warriors. Ruckus would go on to train a thousand new forest activists and take part in the largest coordinated anti-logging campaign in the history of the forest movement.

The Golden Gate Bridge action had been the coming-out party for the new organization. Ruckus was professional, self-confident, and unencumbered by bureaucracy. Rather than just complain about the mass media, which was much more centralized and reactionary than in the past, Ruckus knew how to get headlines. The group excelled at creative confrontation, understood the power of the image and the need to have a simple unifying theme for a successful action.

Of course, not everyone thought that climbing the Golden Gate Bridge was a heroic thing to do. Although we took great pains not to disrupt traffic for any longer than absolutely necessary, and dismantled our barricades after they had been up for only a few minutes, the San Francisco Police decided to halt traffic as they negotiated with the climbers to come down. Angry commuters called in on their cell phones to the radio stations and complained. Much of the San Francisco coverage focused more on the traffic jam than on the redwoods. One radio talk show host called us terrorists and even tried to get the stranded drivers to sue Woody in a class-action lawsuit.

Woody was surprised by the angry response. As the court

proceedings went on, Nancy Pelosi even told him at a house party to, "Stay off my bridge." He was wondering for a moment if he would now be hated in his favorite city. It was needless worry. In a few days, the traffic jam was forgotten, as so many others had been. The lawsuit was never filed, and even the criminal charges were dealt with lightly, resulting in a small fine. But the image of Woody on the bridge is an enduring one. It is the image of an activist inspiring change, not of a terrorist.

Most people don't like to be called terrorists. I have been called an eco-terrorist most of my life, both by the timber, oil, and mining industries—and also by some of my closest allies. I make no apologies. It is said that all is fair in love and war. But even wars have rules, and for a number of reasons I have ruled out violence. I prefer nonviolence, which is the traditional way of doing things in American politics, and this tradition goes back to the Quakers and Henry David Thoreau, and arguably reached its peak during the struggle against segregation in the Deep South under the leadership of Dr. Martin Luther King. Mohandas Gandhi used nonviolent civil disobedience with great skill to drive the British out of India.

King and Gandhi used nonviolence not only because they were morally opposed to violence, but also because they saw it as the better way. When up against a larger, more technologically equipped foe that has a policy of responding to dissent with violence, nonviolence is the only response. The use of violence against a staunch and courageous nonviolent opposition deprives the oppressors of the moral high ground and sways world opinion.

Nonviolence is not a strategy, but a tactic. It is most commonly used when the opposition holds all the power over an important issue and refuses to acknowledge the opposition's voice. Nonviolence serves to address this lopsided balance of power through the willingness to sacrifice one's own freedom in order to persuade or coerce the other party into agreement. Asymmetrical conflicts are not won by strategies, but by tactics, and our struggle is asymmetrical. We are up against a larger, better financed, more politically powerful foe. As the late Brock Evans of the Audubon Society used to tell me, the secret to winning an impossible campaign is endless pressure endlessly applied. My own view is that you need tenacity plus audacity. In order to win against such odds, we need to mobilize public opinion. Victories are rarely strategic—their value is often symbolic. But politicians cannot ignore the opinion of the public forever. The public perception of your chance of winning is even more important than that of the opposition.

As a tactic, the use of violence is corruptive, requires secrecy, and generally isolates its practitioners from the very people and places they wish to serve. I've learned this the hard way, not in some university course.

When I was a roughneck, my driller, Denny Davis, used to tell me, "If you ain't tearing anything up, you ain't getting anything done." He said this after I had literally torched a brand-new desilter unit designed to get abrasive cuttings out of the drilling fluid. The desilter was frozen, and to thaw it out in the 20-below temperatures, Denny told me to pour some diesel fuel on it and light the desilter on fire. It turns out the newer, more expensive units are made out of mostly plastic, and it quickly melted into a smoldering lump. Who knew?

Making mistakes is part of learning, and I destroyed far more oil field equipment by accident when I was working as a roughneck than I ever did when I wasn't on their payroll. In fact, it was my early experience in the oil field that convinced me that you cannot simply burn the bulldozers to stop them. The next Monday morning, they will have a brand-new yellow bulldozer parked in the burnt spot—and along with it a guard. There are better ways to stop the bulldozers, and that is what nonviolence is really all about. It is a legitimate tactic to address the plundering of our environment for short-term profit.

Even though Martin Luther King's birthday is a federal holiday, few people understand how nonviolence works, including the large number of people who practice it. Violent actions by a few can taint a movement as a whole. Indeed, Martin Luther King was blamed for the violence that erupted during the civil rights movement, even though he spent considerable energy to convince people to be nonviolent and never once engaged in political violence.

We might ask why the environmental movement is considered violent by so many Americans, and why it is so easy for the timber industry to portray the movement as violent. One reason is that nobody can agree on what constitutes violence. Is burning a dozer that is scraping an illegal road into a wetland violent? That would depend on whom you talk to. The Boston Tea Party is celebrated as a turning point in the American rebellion against British rule, yet today rioters would be scorned if they protested against a new tax in such a way. The average American has stopped participating in politics. It's difficult even to turn Americans out to the polls to choose a representative to participate in the process for them. Consequently, when an individual or group does demand a seat at the table, it is noticed.

Environmentalists are supposed to behave, and groups like the Sierra Club and the National Wildlife Federation have been fighting the extremist label since their founding, no matter how much they try to play ball. The phony extremist label is their vulnerability. All the opposition has to do is label the Wilderness Society extremist, and the organization will roll belly up, ready to hand over thousands of acres of potential wilderness in an effort to be viewed as reasonable.

Barry Goldwater famously stated that "extremism in the pursuit of liberty is no vice. Moderation in the pursuit of justice is no virtue." He was never afraid of the term extremist, even using it as an advantage. Most of the environmental destruction occurring today is illegal under existing laws. These illegal acts are threatening the viability of our species to exist. It is immoral to stand by and do nothing in the face of such extremism. It is just as immoral to simply go through the motions of opposing these criminal acts without a plan to succeed. One must find a way to stop the mindless poisoning of our air, earth, and water. In this respect, I am an extremist.

Yet I am a nonviolent extremist. I think the health of the environment should be the number one priority of every government in the world, but I am not a revolutionary. I don't really care what kind of government a country has as long as it respects human rights and protects the ecological balance necessary for all life on Earth. Respecting human rights means not hurting anyone; I'm a bit more ambivalent about machines and other inanimate objects. Still, I reject any strategy that relies on property destruction. Though at times it may seem a last line of defense, it ultimately polarizes the issue and alienates supporters.

While the U.S. conservation movement can trace its roots to Henry David Thoreau and John Muir over a century ago, many contend that the modern environmental movement started on

Earth Day 1970. Before then, the term *ecology*, and the complex relationships it describes, were known only to a few activists, politicians, and scientists on university campuses.

From the beginning, the movement did not want to be viewed as extremist, and conservation groups took great pains to appear reasonable. The Sierra Club's support of the Glen Canyon Dam and the Diablo Canyon Nuclear Power Plant in the 1960s demonstrates the point. Yet even though they gave in on these important battles, they never were able to escape the extremist label. Most Americans are inclined to see the Sierra Club as just another special interest group rather than an organization with the task of saving humanity from itself. Outside of the large urban areas, few politicians will seek a Sierra Club endorsement during an election year. Nobody wants to invite charges of being a tree hugger, or in the case of presidential candidate Al Gore, Mr. Ozone. An unwavering commitment to the environment is not a political asset in most elections.

During the struggle against segregation in the South, most major civil rights organizations not only supported nonviolent civil disobedience, but made sure there was money to fund it, too. Today, only a few environmental groups support the use of nonviolent civil disobedience, and, with the exception of Greenpeace, none of the big groups do.

Al Gore has called for young people to sit in front of the bulldozers at the site of new coal-fired power plants, yet he will neither join them nor send them any of the hundreds of millions of dollars he has raised. Only one thing can account for this: He is afraid of being called an extremist. Barry Goldwater and Martin Luther King Jr. had no such fear.

Without full support for a campaign of civil disobedience

from the major environmental groups, there is little hope that the current feeble efforts to prevent even more climate change will have any chance of success. It took the major environmental groups decades to come out against logging in the old-growth forests. The nonviolent campaigns by Earth First! and other grassroots groups across the country finally forced the hand of Big Green when their members began to voice support for such campaigns.

Though Big Green didn't support the nonviolent protests, they reaped huge benefits when saving old-growth forests became mainstream and profitable. Meanwhile, it was the grassroots direct action effort that stopped logging in ancient forests, by spending day after day, year after year, blocking the illegal roads. It was the grassroots groups that filed the lawsuits and made the headlines. Only afterwards did a few of the big environmental groups come around to the position that all logging in wilderness and ancient forests should be ended immediately. By that time, 95 percent of ancient forests in the United States had already been logged.

Civil disobedience is always an extreme measure. In the case of the ancient forests, it was called for by the fact that the government refused to enforce its own laws and that a valuable natural resource was being destroyed, resulting in a mass extinction of plants and animals. Sure you've heard about the spotted owl, but there are thousands of other species that are equally imperiled. To destroy their only habitat is a crime under U.S. law. Something had to be done, and done quickly, to force the government agencies to follow their own laws—just as something has to be done now to end the mining, drilling, and burning of fossil fuels.

Another thing I am often called is an outside agitator. Again, I make no apologies. My phone never rings unless an environmental group is desperate. By that time, they are no longer worried about being called extremist. The group will do anything, short of violence, to save whichever remnant of nature they have been fighting for. It is this very desperation that makes them powerful. Unafraid, they can wage a campaign that not only inflicts pain on their opponents, but also changes the political landscape through high-profile confrontation.

It wasn't the anger that effected change, but rather the commitment to creating change, the nobility of the suffering, and the depth of the love for nature. A strong code of ethics is essential to a successful nonviolent movement. Just as a soldier who goes off to war knows that she may be injured or even killed, the nonviolent soldier understands that risks must be taken and sacrifices must be made in pursuit of a higher goal. Every soldier is an extremist.

Like all warfare, nonviolent civil disobedience requires training, discipline, and sacrifice. Basically, that's what we outside agitators do. I have been training activists for civil disobedience for upwards of twenty-five years, and I am still doing it today. The kind of training we do isn't taught at the university, there are few useful guide books, and only a few organizations are dedicated to its successful use. The key to the successful use of civil disobedience is an understanding of its history. In the history of its use are the lessons learned in previous campaigns. Only seasoned campaigners truly understand this, and our ranks are small. Those of us who do this sort of thing travel frequently.

The Ruckus Society grabbed national attention with the Golden Gate Bridge action, but the idea for Ruckus took root as

Twilly Cannon and I were playing a game of pool, looking out the window from the Opal Creek Lodge into the ancient forests of the Cascades. It was the spring of 1995.

A meeting was going on in the lodge, but Twilly and I had long since lost interest. Gathered in the room, sitting in a circle, were the key organizers of the grassroots forest movement, a scrappy bunch of veteran Earth First! activists who had been the only line of defense between the loggers and the ancient forest since the eighties. The meeting, bogged down in process, was dragging on. Usually the process produced scraps of paper with the names of new committees that would report back to central leadership the next time the group got together. I had been to many such meetings, the same people always showed up eager to be heard on just about any subject.

This meeting was a little different, though. The tree huggers were mad and not sure exactly what to do. In 1994, four million acres of western forests burned. The Forest Service response to the event was to create a false forest-health crisis. The solution? Lawless logging without public process in old-growth roadless tracts, aimed to resuscitate the forest that had done just fine before the Forest Service started punching in roads and cutting timber. Sounds like environmental conspiracy, right? Nah, just your tax dollars at work.

If you want to suspend environmental laws in pursuit of old growth, you have to do it real quiet-like. The Forest Service attached an amendment to the recisions bill for the 1995 U.S. budget. The move, known as the controversial Salvage Rider, would increase logging in burned lands without providing an option for administrative appeals on the final decision, a cornerstone of the National Environmental Protection Act.

By nixing the appeal process, the Forest Service effectively

cut out opposition from the grassroots watchdogs whose lawyers were knocking the agency's socks off. More dastardly was
an order in the Salvage Rider to rerelease green, old-growth
timber sales that had been scrapped due to environmental
concerns in 1990. That addition to the Salvage Rider was added
from Section 318 of the 1990 Appropriations Bill. Section 318
infuriated the tree huggers more than anything else. Hell hath
no fury like an environmentalist's scorn of hard-fought-for environmental laws, summarily suspended.

Without the appeals process, the Forest Service had to be
trusted to follow federal environmental laws such as the Endangered Species Act, the Clean Water Act, the National Forest
Management Act, and the Wilderness Act. The Forest Service
had an atrocious track record for complying with these laws.
Why would they follow the law now?

During the early 1990s, most of the really bad timber sales
occurring in ancient forests were being stopped by lawsuits
and legal appeals. As a result, many of the organizations had
shifted from direct action to research and litigation, using the
Forest Service's own byzantine regulations to thwart the timber industry plans to enter the remaining roadless forests.
After leaving the direct-action front lines in the late eighties,
many first-wave Earth Firsters went back to school to get law
degrees. They filed aggressive lawsuits and set new precedents
that made it difficult for the Forest Service to sell timber. The
combined effect of these lawsuits had stopped logging over
wide swaths of the nation's forests. This caused them to be
labeled—you guessed it—extremists.

In fact, it had been the very success of the lawsuits that
was causing the current problem. Logging had been reduced
significantly on the National Forest by a succession of U.S.

Federal Court decisions that defined more narrowly the conditions under which logging can take place on federally owned lands. Clear-cutting became known as a failed forestry technique. Road building was deemed a dismal economic and ecological failure. Wildlife and their habitat were gaining inherent rights to exist. This produced a predictable howl of protest from the timber industry and its political allies.

Thus began the "forest health crisis," the "we have to destroy the forest in order to save it" strategy that convinced much of the American public that nature could not be trusted and that drastic human intervention was needed in order to prevent catastrophic fires and massive die-offs from insects and disease. In fact, the Salvage Rider allowed the timber industry to get away with brazen theft of public property, exempt from environmental lawsuits. All the Freddies needed to do now was label any controversial timber sale necessary for forest health, and nothing could stop them.

On July 27, 1995, President Bill Clinton would sign the Salvage Rider, attached to a budget bill containing financial aid for victims of the Oklahoma City bombing and for war-torn Bosnia. He did what no Republican had been able to do for the last twelve years—an end run around all applicable environmental laws, opening up the remaining unprotected wilderness on public lands to increased logging.

The group of forest activists at the meeting at Opal Creek knew Clinton would sign the bill. Over the years, they had always found many things on which to disagree. One thing that united them today was the grim realization that in order to have any chance of holding back this new assault on the forest by the Clinton Administration, they would need to return to the barricades—and in greater numbers than ever before. It would take a widespread coordinated campaign of civil disobedience to get the public sufficiently outraged to demand a halt to the destruction of the last roadless national forest land.

The problem here, as Twilly and I saw it, was that the attendants of this meeting weren't ready to return to the dust and mud of the forest blockades. Most of the people at the meeting had been arrested during the previous waves of civil disobedience that began in 1983 on Bald Mountain. But the last time a mass civil disobedience action was attempted was in Northern California, and it took over ten years to build up to it. Civil disobedience was at this time still a very important tactic in the battle to stop logging, but most of these actions were small and in remote locations.

Immediately the cry was to go out and block the bulldozers. I knew from experience that this was not likely to happen just because a handful of disgruntled environmentalists called for it. A campaign of this sort needed to be organized by experienced campaigners or it would peter out and be politically ineffective. When participants in a civil disobedience campaign are unprepared for the rigors and sacrifice required for a successful nonviolent campaign, collapse is inevitable. The repercussions of civil disobedience can be severe. They include jail, fines, lawsuits, even public outrage that includes violence or threats of violence from the opposition. It is no walk in the park, nor should it be. If your action is justifiable, the campaign will eventually withstand the test of public scrutiny.

Protesters can always expect to be outnumbered by loggers. Violence from loggers is the norm, not the exception, and every demonstrator risks injury and serious criminal charges when they blockade a road. These risks should be accepted without complaint, and through the worst of it, activists should remain peaceful and respectful to timber workers. They deserve our sympathy, though we are objects of their animosity.

Over the years, Earth First! developed a crew of expert itinerant nonviolence trainers who were also adept in the tactics necessary to actually slow down the logging, as most of them had little patience for actions that were merely symbolic. The currency for an Earth First! action was downtime, and the longer the project was shut down, the more it was deemed successful. This, of course, brought even more retribution from the loggers and cops, and many Earth Firsters had gotten used to long jail sentences, large fines, extended probation, and civil lawsuits to recover the cost of the protest. Clearly it is hard to convince a large group of people to make such sacrifices. As a result, most Earth First! actions were small and extremely dangerous.

Greenpeace, too, had a training program. For Greenpeace, news coverage was the currency by which all actions were judged, but they also had the goal of causing as much havoc as possible to achieve downtime, in which they also placed great currency. While there were many similarities between the Earth First! approach and that of Greenpeace, there were also many differences.

Greenpeace was flush with cash, had a million members, staff lawyers, and media representatives. While they were often arrested, they were seldom held for long, due to coordinated protest from their membership and allied politicians. Since most Greenpeace action teams were international, the prosecutors also had to endure the protests of the activist's home government. In the end, however, it was Greenpeace's sterling reputation for nonviolence that made them powerful and their activists hard to jail.

Earth Firsters not only had little funding, but they were, thanks to their reputation for violence, unfundable. Earth Firsters often paid for the entire action with their own meager resources. Earth Firsters rarely had criminal lawyers, either using public defenders or representing themselves. They often refused to leave the jail unless their own conditions—such as no fine or probation—were met.

Media was another area where the two groups differed. Earth Firsters needed the element of surprise to achieve maximum downtime, and since the protest sites were so remote, often there was no news media present at the protests. This resulted in a lack of mainstream photos and footage. Such a detail would be considered unacceptable for a Greenpeace action. Still, Earth First! usually received more overall media attention, mostly due to the relentless pace of their campaigns, sometimes pulling off multiple actions in a week at the same location.

Much of the media Earth First! received was propelled more by the violent reaction of the timber industry and the efforts of the county prosecutor's office than by the actions themselves. A key law enforcement tactic was intimidation. This approach never worked on Earth Firsters, who refused to back down to threats of jail time and fines. It followed in the footsteps of Thoreau. When asked by Waldo Emerson what he was doing in jail for refusing to pay a poll tax in protest of the Mexican War, Thoreau responded, "The question is what are you doing out there?" Earth Firsters would initiate effective jail protests, and other Earth Firsters would travel to the area to blockade the road and attempt to fill the jails. This all provided plenty of conflict for the news media to cover.

Twilly and I had both been involved in training Greenpeacers and others since the eighties. By 1990, with the help of the many trainers in our network, we developed a comprehensive program to prepare campaigners for the rigors of direct action. It encompassed all aspects of planning and staging successful direct actions. By the end of several beers and games of pool, we decided it was time to revive the program and adapt it to the needs of the campaign to stop the Salvage Rider.

To mount such an offensive, we would need money. We quickly identified a few eccentric wealthy donors and a couple of foundations that were willing to give us a chance. This included the Lazar Foundation and the Turner Foundation, controlled by the family of media mogul Ted Turner, which was then being directed by my old boss at Greenpeace, Peter Bahouth. It was Bahouth who had overseen the development of the Greenpeace action team in the eighties, and the growth of Greenpeace into one of the nation's largest environmental groups. The Turner Foundation, under Bahouth's "Thin Green Blanket of Love" strategy, had been disbursing millions of dollars to the front-line environmental groups across the country. No one knew the landscape better than he did, or what we were up against.

The first Ruckus camp was held in the Cascade Range near the town of Detroit, Oregon, in the summer of 1995. We enrolled eighty students, brought them to the camp, and spent an entire week in rigorous training and education, conducted by the most experienced activists in the country. Afterwards, a large number of these activists set up a camp in the drainage of Warner Creek, Oregon, where the U.S. Forest Service planned to log old growth using the Salvage Rider.

Like the Cove/Mallard campaign in central Idaho, the Warner Creek campaign would prove to be an epic struggle. Ultimately the struggle was victorious. Not only was it a success for Warner Creek, but a huge symbolic victory for the forest protection movement as well. We had gotten our mojo back. While other environmental groups were wringing their hands and complaining that they had been locked out of the courtroom, Earth First!, Greenpeace, the Rainforest Action Network, and hundreds of smaller groups took the fight onto the ground in forests across the country.

Similar blockades broke out all over the West, and Ruckus coordinators, who by now numbered a few hundred, traveled about the country offering assistance. Across the West, one uprising after the next occurred whenever the Forest Service tried to execute a "forest health" clear-cut. Although the Sierra Club forbade any of their paid staff to participate in any of these actions, I was arrested in direct actions with Brock Evans of the Audubon Society, former Indiana congressman Jim Jontz, and Andy Kerr of the Oregon Natural Resource Council, the state's powerhouse grassroots conservation organization.

Kerr and I kicked off the campaign by getting arrested in Oregon Senator Bob Packwood's office; Packwood was a timber beast and huge proponent of the Salvage Rider. This was before the Rider was even voted on. As the campaign went on, thousands more were arrested and the Forest Service would back down on one timber sale after another. It eventually withdrew most of the Salvage Rider forest-health timber sales. In 1996, the law expired and was not renewed.

By 1999, Ruckus had grown into a larger organization and had moved its offices from Missoula, Montana, to Berkeley, California. By that time, I had resigned as director and hired John Sellers as my replacement. We recruited a board of directors, and I moved to Washington, D.C., to work with Ralph Nader's organization Citizens for Responsive Law.

I was placed beneath Nader's chief of staff, John Richard, and former Greenpeace staffer Ned Daly. Daly, Bahouth, Randy Hayes, and I had started a D.C. think tank called the Resource Conservation Alliance, devoted to ending the use of old-growth forest products by promoting alternatives and focusing on the nontimber values of natural forests. The job involved much research, writing, speaking, conference organizing, and alliance-building with like-minded businesses and organizations.

In the end, the Salvage Rider was brought down by the sheer weight of the protests from the grassroots showdown in the forests. We were locked out of the courtroom, so we took the case to the only jury that really mattered—the court of public opinion. This was a campaign that could only have been won by mass civil disobedience, as all other means had been exhausted.

The next campaign for Ruckus would take the organization out of the forests and into the streets of the cities, attracting a new wave of young activists who would attempt to rewrite the rules for nonviolent civil disobedience. This experiment would end with the terror attacks of 9/11 and the advent of war in Afghanistan and Iraq.

11

Battle in Seattle

By 1999, the Ruckus Society's success was having its effect on the organization. They had received large amounts of media attention, both broadcast and print. Trainers and organizers were active across the country, organizing on a variety of issues. Upwards of a thousand activists had been hosted at eleven training camps, representing a variety of groups and issues. Internationally, Ruckus had attracted participants from the Tibetan and Burmese human-rights movements, the Tarahumara in the Copper Canyon of rural Mexico, the First Nations of Canada in the coastal rain forests of British Columbia, and activists from England, Germany, Russia, Bulgaria, Nigeria, Korea, and Taiwan. On top of that, Ruckus was actively protesting old-growth logging in Canada and Mexico.

This success, of course, also had its downside. Ruckus began to see itself as the vanguard of a new movement, one that was rewriting the rules on civil protest. In the process, they

abandoned a century of nonviolent tradition and started talking much more militantly. They equated their struggle with
those of the Zapatistas, the Palestinians, and other armed
groups fighting imperialism. They were no longer interested in
forests or biological diversity, believing such issues could be
solved only through the overthrow of capitalism and the creation of a new government. Slowly, the Buckaroos who hadn't
been purged in the California revolution of the early nineties
were leaving or being forced out with accusations that they
were old, white, and misanthropic.

Ruckus would reach its zenith in November 1999 at the
World Trade Organization meeting in Seattle. The WTO had
long been the whipping boy of the anti-globalization movement, a collective that even its most articulate adherents in the
United States had trouble describing. The movement meant
different things to different people. Globalization was depicted
as the cause for every social and environmental problem we
were facing. People were coming out of the woodwork to protest in Seattle on a variety of issues, from the protection of sea
turtles to ending poverty in undeveloped countries. The United
Steel Workers planned to attend with twenty thousand members, opposing the shipping of jobs overseas. Mass civil disobedience was called for by a number of environmental and
human rights organizations. It would be a circus.

I attended a meeting in San Francisco to discuss plans for
the big demonstration. One of the people at the meeting was a
young man by the name of David Solnit, representing a new
group called the Direct Action Network, whose members would
be key organizers for the mass civil disobedience planned for
Seattle. Solnit laid out a plan of mobile civil disobedience,
where roving bands of anarchists would attempt to block traf-

fic and keep the WTO delegates from attending the WTO meeting. He said that it was modeled on the strategy used in Miami at the Republican Convention in 1972. I'm guessing he wasn't born by then.

I had been quiet for most of the meeting, but this was too much.

"David," I said. "Yes, the tactic was used in Miami. I was there. We had a riot and Nixon got elected. I don't know if you want a riot. But you will have a riot. Trust me."

The meeting went on for another hour or so, and everyone looked at me like I was some kind of dinosaur. I had hoped to have more success in questioning the wisdom of the risky roving-band strategy. Ruckus was planning an action camp just before the November WTO meeting. Very little training occurred. Instead, there were dozens of organizers on hand to argue every possible angle in a broad consensus process that included everyone who attended.

No one was in charge. No one would be accountable. Any group could do what they wanted, as long as no one was hurt. Property destruction wasn't even discussed. Few present thought any would occur. The anarchists were now in charge of the protest. There would be no leaders, few rules, and many different approaches. It would be a free-for-all.

I didn't want any part in the event. I'd been to a lot of marches. I don't see large protests as particularly effective. In the years since the sixties, most of them have taken on a cele-bratory, even festive atmosphere, accompanied by giant pup-pets, stilt walkers, and drums. Marches like this are typically followed by speeches. The microphone is dominated by the most extreme groups, who make all sorts of demands on all sorts of progressive issues. I tired of these events in the 1960s and never once saw them have a serious impact on anything. They were more parade than protest, more speech than action, a convergence of the believers, by the believers, for the believers.

When thousands of activists converge on one location and nothing happens, the movement risks losing its credibility. The number of planning meetings required for a mass mobilization is quite atrocious, and the number of egos to deal with is more so. In my experience, it is usually a waste of time. Large demonstrations didn't stop the Vietnam War. The war broke under its own weight.

In 1963, when the March on Washington was being organized by the civil rights movement, almost everyone outside the movement was convinced that there would be violence despite the assurances of Martin Luther King Jr. and all the other organizers that it would be peaceful. Churches, unions, and grassroots organizations all pooled their meager resources to mobilize memberships, raise money, charter buses, and rent motel rooms and campgrounds. They had a strong leadership, rigid discipline, and a strategy to force federal action on the issue of segregation. King was leading an army, not a mob. He never would have suggested that the marchers should shut down the nation's capital.

I began to get fed up with the WTO planning process. I had made plans to run the Chinko River in Central Africa in an effort to bring conservation to the region. Growing more and more jaded by the day, I ditched out on the planning and went to Africa. In September of 1999, I spent a month in the Central African Republic on an expedition to make the first descent of the Chinko River by boat. We made the journey, but I came back with a bad case of drug-resistant malaria. Too weak to travel, I stayed in Berkeley and missed the Ruckus training. I would have to sit out the WTO meeting as well. I would be watching it on television like millions of people around the world. The only difference was that I had a strange sense of déjà vu.

Nobody has been able to agree on how many people turned out in Seattle that day. The media originally reported thirty thousand. It was easily over one hundred thousand. The first morning of the meeting, November 30, the mass descended on downtown and paralyzed the infrastructure of Seattle. It was an epic gathering of historic proportions. The crowd was peaceful and diverse in its age, ethnicity, and political background. Sea turtles stood next to hard hats. People in the streets had shut down the city. The cops had taken defensive positions, setting up small perimeters at certain intersections. Around them, a sea of people simply existed. There wasn't much for a protester to do, as it was hard to move anywhere in a thirty-block radius. Around 10 A.M., the cops rained the first tear gas canisters on protesters sitting in the intersections.

I was watching FOX News when the first tear gas canister was fired into the crowd. It was at that time that I was sure I would be watching the first large nonracial riot since the sixties. Sure enough, it all played out right on my television screen. Soon, any discussion of the WTO and the problems with globalization were buried beneath the weight of hundreds of tear gas canisters. All the protesters could talk about was the conduct of the Seattle Police Department, which was now attacking protesters all over the city. In response, the small numbers of the Black Block, named for their black bandannas and shirts, pulled out their hammers and dropped every corporate window and ATM in the city. As night fell, fires erupted in the street.

Though the Black Block numbered less than 1 percent of the crowd, they were spaced out and went big with their actions. The sea turtles and the hard hats were now side by side with vandals who were trying to spark some sort of urban uprising. The sea turtles and hard hats had not signed on for urban uprising. Now the media was bogged down in claims by the police that the protesters were violent. If the nonviolent front line had been held, the police would have been in a deep hole, as they attacked the crowd before the Black Block struck.

The Battle in Seattle became the biggest story of the year. It resulted in hundreds of arrests and gave new momentum to the anarchist movement. The anarchists' actions commanded the focus of the news coverage. Images of black-clad, bandanna-wearing anarchists throwing rocks at Starbucks windows came to define the event, pushing any other issue by the wayside. In the process, a great wedge was driven between groups who believed that the WTO had been successful in shutting down the meeting, and those who were now going to be much more cautious about joining any coalition with the anarchists, who would make no apologies for their actions.

The riot forced the canceling of the opening ceremonies. The city was essentially under martial law. The meeting failed, but over a disagreement between rich and poor countries over agricultural subsidies—not because of the riots. The work of the WTO and the advance of globalization went ahead unimpeded. Meanwhile, the organizers hailed the riot as a monumental success. They became intoxicated with the media attention they received and were absolutely sure that future demonstrations would be larger and more militant. The tactics had worked! They would not be changed.

The Battle in Seattle wasn't all bad.

"We have gotten more attention on the World Trade Organization in the last forty-eight hours than we have in the last twenty years we have been working on it," Friends of the Earth's Brent Blackwelder told me. True enough.

A large part of the antiglobalization movement in the United States had focused on the environmental impacts of globalization, such as the ecological cost of large hydroelectric dams, strip mines, and power plants. This new movement was mainly anticorporate in tone, staunchly anticapitalist in spirit, and antiauthoritarian in ideology. It was a revolutionary movement, one dedicated to overthrowing the established order. The only problem was that nobody could agree on what to replace it with. Ultimately, the movement turned into a conflict between police and protesters. Each complained about the other's tactics. Mostly, the issue of the global finance system had been lost in the squabble over the riots.

After the WTO riot, John Sellers was quoted in *Mother Jones*, a prominent progressive monthly magazine, as saying, "I make a distinction between violence and destruction of property. Violence to me is against living things. But inanimate objects? I think you can be destructive, you can use vandalism strategically. It may be violence under the law, but I just don't think it's violence." In another interview in the *New Left Review*, he went even further to ally Ruckus to the increasingly volatile street protests that had been held in America's largest cities. "Anarchism has got a really bad rap, like communism."

Ruckus's problem now was that they believed in their own media. They thought the Black Block had become the cutting edge of the protest movement and did not want to be seen as opposed to the anarchists on tactics.

Here was the problem with the anarchists, though: It was

largely an intellectual, white, middle-class youth movement with little support outside coffee shops in college towns and urban centers. Their lifestyles were strange and alien to most Americans. The anarchists themselves were really not at fault. They were never that many in number. The romantic notions of the environmental and human rights groups held that the anarchists were reasonable and could be managed. In reality, many anarchists had come to the conclusion that violence was the only solution. The reaction of the Seattle police just served to reinforce their ideology.

It was Ruckus that taught the anti-globalists how to lock down for a blockade. Lockdowns are extremely useful when a small group of protesters wants to maximize impact. But when used in the downtown of a major city, it wreaks havoc on the traffic and affects the entire population. The Seattle police had no experience with these sorts of tactics. The police chief had attended peace marches in the sixties and thought that he knew what to expect. The failure to establish good communications with the police and set some ground rules meant that the police had no idea what they were up against. They, too, lacked the training for such an exercise. When the blockades went up and shut down the downtown businesses, law enforcement was under pressure to act. No one had ever used these tactics to disrupt a city. In Miami, there were no lockboxes, and police would simply haul the protesters peacefully into the waiting buses. The protesters in Seattle were not removed easily. When the first tear gas grenade exploded, it was too late to do anything about it.

The result was a police riot, more in line with the 1968 Democratic National Convention, the other melee that helped to elect Richard Nixon to the presidency. The organizers of the

WTO protest would continue to argue long after the WTO riots were over that it was only a few demonstrators who were violent, and that the rest were peaceful. This was true. But it does ignore the fact that many of the campaigners condoned the participation of the anarchists. It was the "mobile civil disobedience" strategy and "diversity of tactics" policy that led to police violence in Seattle.

Large mass protests, as both Gandhi and Martin Luther King learned the hard way, need discipline and focus, or the demonstration can easily get out of control, making it difficult to attract new people. Eventually protests will dwindle as the core group of radicals moves on to something else. The Seattle organizers didn't know this lesson and readied to take their show on the road, complete with the Black Block anarchists. The next stop was scheduled for Washington, D.C., for the April 16, 2000, meeting of the World Bank.

The twentieth century would come to an end without a Y2K breakdown. It was an election year, and the World Bank was returning to Washington, D.C., for their biannual meeting at the Sheraton Hotel. Once again, the anti-globalists would be calling for mass civil disobedience. Only this time, the activists claimed that their goal was not just to shut down the World Bank meeting, but to paralyze the entire capital with blockades of bridges, tunnels, and freeways. Washington, D.C., cops have more experience with street protests than do any police force in the country. They were put on high alert and given new riot gear. The city felt like it was under siege. Nobody knew what to expect. The city's residents, usually supportive of demonstrations, were unfriendly. When the protesters began to arrive in early April, the city was buzzing, large areas of the city were cordoned off from the public. Most of the delegates, learning their lesson from the Seattle protests, arrived early in buses that were escorted by the police.

The World Bank meeting was surrounded, but only by a thin line of blockaders, and most delegates had no trouble getting inside. The protests continued for most of the day, with confrontations with police breaking out here and there. For the most part, the protesters were contained. There was very little violence or property damage. In the days leading up to the protest, the Washington, D.C., Police Department had made a series of preemptive arrests at various locations where organizers assembled. In one instance, they seized a protester's giant puppet. As in Seattle, the story soon turned into one between police and protesters, with the cops calling the protesters violent, and the protesters calling the cops fascists. The World Bank meeting went ahead without delay.

The result was somewhat anticlimactic, and nothing much changed. When it was over, it seemed unnecessary. It was just a bunch of skinny white kids who had too much time on their hands. From Washington, D.C., this unruly mob went on to assemble at both the Republican and Democratic National Conventions. Then it was on to San Diego to protest at a convention on genetic engineering. Things started petering out. Then terrorists struck the World Trade Center in New York City. The party came to an abrupt halt.

War came to the country. Afghanistan, and then Iraq, diverted the movement's attention from globalization to protesting against the war. Of course, large segments from both sides of the aisle of American society, including celebrities and politicians, were already against the war, and the protests did little to change the numbers. The protesters had no plan to stop the violence in Iraq and Afghanistan. They only called for U.S.

troops to pull out and let the region sink into real anarchy. The American public, for the most part, was not buying it.

Anarchists totally ruled Ruckus now, and purged anyone who disagreed with them. This left the organization with a staff of young, inexperienced, and very ideological trainers who were unprepared for the backlash that followed 9/11. Indeed they were now convinced that all elections would be stolen, more wars would be started, and all the dissenters would be rounded up and put in camps. They were paralyzed with fear. It was in this atmosphere of fear and repression that the Earth Liberation Front would draw new strength, as some of the frustrated anarchists became more desperate for results.

12

Green Scare—The Brief and Brutal Career of the ELF

It would be wrong to categorize the large number of anarchists who made up the anti-globalization movement as ineffective. What made this group unpredictable and unaccountable also made them powerful. Totally convinced of their righteousness, they were dedicated and committed to a life of resistance. They traveled far and wide to participate in demonstrations. Many activists would go on from the Battle in Seattle to become leaders in the new environmental movement.

Anarchists can be handy. No movement for positive social change in the recent history of this country could have succeeded without anarchists. Indeed Martin Luther King Jr. faced the same problem with these romantic, ideological anti-authoritarians as the environmental groups did in Seattle. At first he referred to them as kooks, but later came to realize that they were a useful, if unruly, group. Many anarchists traveled to the Deep South to fight segregation, enduring hardships and danger.

There was a critical difference in the new breed of anarchist who joined the environmental ranks in the late 1990s. The new anarchists lacked a commitment to, and an understanding of, nonviolence. The peaceniks and civil rights workers held a deeply spiritual belief in nonviolence, something the anti-globalists lacked. The anarchists wanted to build a broad-based and diverse movement, but there was no room for anyone who did not conform to their rigid set of principles and worldview. The food was vegan, the music hip-hop, and clothes black. Tattoos and piercing were required. Nice clothes were deemed suspicious. It was hard to see how anyone could expect a broad-based, diverse movement to develop along these lines.

If that wasn't enough, another development would further add to the anxiety of the anarchist protesters. After almost ten years of fruitless searching, a break in the case of the Earth Liberation Front resulted in the arrest of fourteen members. They were charged with a string of arsons across the country that caused several million dollars in damage. The knee-jerk reaction from the anarchists was that all these defendants were somehow innocent. The roundup of so many well-known activists had to be part of a government plot to wipe out dissent. They dubbed the effort Operation Green Scare, comparing the arrests to the Red Scare when thousands of innocent people were harassed and jailed for their perceived links to the American Communist Party.

The ELF had been very busy from 1998 to 2004. The most spectacular crime was the torching of Vail Resort, a ski area in Colorado. The arson cost an estimated $20 million in damage and made front-page news worldwide. The ELF was very active, and their targets ranged from housing developments, SUV dealerships, slaughterhouses, tree farms, and logging operations. This triggered one of the biggest manhunts in the history of the FBI, and earned the ELF a title as America's most dangerous domestic terrorist organization.

But who was the ELF? No one seemed to know, even within the environmental movement. I had assumed that the ELF actions were done by various unconnected autonomous groups connected only by arson and their hatred for large corporations destroying the Earth. It turned out I was wrong, and I would discover this when my friend Bill Rodgers committed suicide in an Arizona jail after his arrest as the mastermind of the ELF.

I first met Rodgers, who went by the name Avalon, when he showed up at the Cove/Mallard base camp on Ramon's land in Dixie, Idaho. He chose his forest name after the 1982 fantasy novel *The Mists of Avalon* by Marion Zimmer Bradley. The novel retells the legend of King Arthur from a feminist viewpoint. It was a book he carried with him wherever he went, urging others to read it. Small and thin, sporting a reddish beard and short hair, quiet and soft-spoken, he didn't stand out much from the many other activists who had come to Dixie to work on the Cove/Mallard campaign. He busied himself mostly with taking new recruits deep into the wilderness beyond base camp and showing them the proposed logging sites. These hikes usually motivated the recruits into taking some kind of action. At Cove/Mallard base camp, that meant blocking the bulldozers, log trucks, and chain saws.

Avalon also had a darker side, one that I was totally unaware of until his arrest and suicide. Avalon had recruited a cell for a group he called the Earth Liberation Front. Patterned after the much older Animal Liberation Front, it shared many of its ideals and tactics, including the use of arson and property destruction to achieve its goal of stopping the destruction of the planet. It was this core group that was responsible for the majority of the ELF arsons.

As it would turn out, most of the ELF defendants had attended at least one Ruckus training camp. At least I had comfort in knowing that we did not train them to commit violent acts. In fact, we strongly discouraged it. In the Cove/Mallard campaign, property destruction was forbidden. In Cove/Mallard, Avalon and his band of eco-guerillas complied, but elsewhere they were up to something altogether more violent than anything that had ever been done in the name of the environment before.

When the ELF was finally rounded up, I received many requests to help them with their legal problems. I was willing to lend advice, as overzealous federal prosecutors have a reputation for using scant evidence and creating larger conspiracies to look more effective at fighting terrorism. But there were some big problems with their defense.

None of the ELF members admitted guilt, and thus were not portrayed as captured soldiers. The defendants had separate attorneys, and separate agendas. There was another legal defense team not affiliated with any of the defendants, but rather focused on the constitutional rights of all radical environmentalists. In their view, the FBI was criminalizing dissent and targeting the radical environmental movement with phony charges in order to harass and immobilize them. This would prove to be pure fantasy.

Normally when terrorists are apprehended, they use any

opportunity they can get to drive home their message, whatever it may be. In this case, none of the ELF defendants wanted to admit that there was an ELF, much less that they were in it. The legal-defense team pursued a strategy to paint the FBI as overzealous. They said the agency was rounding up innocent people in an attempt to close the Vail case and deter any future ELF violence. On top of that, they were disrupting the movement and rescuing themselves from the humiliating situation after a decade of failing to stop what they called the most dangerous domestic terrorist group in the United States (all fourteen of them) that was operating right under the government's nose. After all, the FBI long ago infiltrated the militant environmental groups and knew all the key players.

The defendants who were arrested were well-known anarchists and radical environmentalists who traveled the protest circuit, attending demonstrations across the country. I had met them all at one time or another, and knew some of them quite well. Even so, I was more surprised than anyone when the warrants were issued. I had discussed this issue with several of the accused without ever suspecting they were involved.

I argued against this kind of action for the reasons that were now becoming obvious. With the arrest of the fourteen, the ELF not only dropped off the map, but now fourteen good organizers would spend a significant portion of their lives in prison or on the lam. Worst of all, in order to receive reduced sentences, some defendants reportedly cooperated with the prosecution—even to the point of wearing wires to tape incriminating conversations initiated to gather evidence the FBI lacked.

The legal-defense team stuck with the Green Scare theme throughout the trial and proceeded to scare the bejeezus out of everyone who was not already terrified of the federal government, making the Green Scare a self-fulfilling prophecy. In no instance have I seen or suspected a coordinated attempt by the federal government to disrupt the environmental movement. When disruption of the environmental movement is instigated, it's usually done by a private corporation, or sometimes the Forest Service acting alone.

The Green Scare was a sham. There were no heroes in this story. Not even Avalon would become a martyr for the movement. There was not enough support amongst environmentalists for a campaign of violence to sustain an underground guerilla force. The defendants never overcame their political isolation even after they were apprehended. It became obvious by the time the last ELF defendants were sentenced in Eugene in October of 2006 that the ELF had failed to produce anything beyond banner headlines and undue alarm. In the end, it changed nothing, and the energy expended could have been much better used building a broad-based and disciplined environmental movement.

The effect of the whole ELF and WTO debacles was in my view mostly negative. First, the anti-globalization activists belittled and ignored over a hundred years of nonviolent tradition by refusing to condemn massive property destruction, all of this in an effort to embrace the anarchists who had their own agenda. Then the ELF took it a step further, insisting that property destruction and violence were necessary. In the end, the ELF and the anti-globalists were not prepared to make the ultimate sacrifice. They wanted everything the easy way. When they got caught, they folded their cards, denouncing violence and admitting their mistakes. In a sense, they had gotten religion, the hard way.

As a nonviolent movement to reverse climate change develops, it should take to heart the lessons of the WTO and the ELF. The last year has seen the spread of protests against coal-fired power plants in several states and rising unrest in the coal fields. While violence can create headlines, headlines alone cannot sustain a movement. Movements are built from the bottom up, with care and patience, and with openness and honesty—but most of all, with courage.

In the end, it takes more courage to sit in front of a bulldozer than it does to burn one.

13

Appalachian Destruction— The Fight Ahead

Climate change is here. If you are not yet convinced of this, you are now in the minority. The changes we are experiencing are just the tip of the iceberg. A rise in temperature, melting ice caps, rising sea levels, failing crops, and mass extinction are all well documented and under way. Regardless of what we do now, the world our grandchildren will inherit will be very different from the world we have known all our lives.

Is there any good news?

If this dark cloud has any silver lining, it is that people are waking up to the problem, and more and more of them are taking action. There are many changes that must be made to avert the worst effects of climate change. The first and most important step is to stop using coal energy. It will not be an easy task. If we fail, we will slip into a catastrophe of unprecedented proportions. It must also be mentioned that even without the looming threat of climate change, we are in big trouble.

The skies, oceans, and forests have been under siege for centuries and show signs of significant decline. Extinction rates are already climbing to a rate one thousand times greater than what is expected naturally, with scientists predicting that one-fourth of all mammal species are in danger. Our soils are being depleted at an ever faster rate, threatening our food supply.

Not everyone is convinced that it is too late for action. Many believe that there is still time to act. Former Vice President Al Gore has called on young people to engage in civil disobedience to prevent the construction of any new coal-fired power plants. Why this should be left to the young is a bit puzzling, as the young bear little responsibility for the situation we are in. But I am convinced that ranks of the youth are what we need to move forward.

Why?

Because even though we live in a democracy, and a majority of people favor converting to cleaner sources of energy, the politicians are simply too addicted to the money that the coal industry contributes to their campaigns. Opposing coal costs politicians crucial votes in coal-mining states. This is not unlike the situation that civil-rights activists faced in the Deep South during the struggle against segregation laws. Most people thought it was well past time to repeal the unconstitutional and immoral Jim Crow laws. But politicians in the South could not stand up to the segregationists and still maintain public office.

This is what led segregationist George Wallace to declare after losing an election for the governor's office in Alabama in 1958 that he would "never be out-niggered again." Later in life, Wallace sought redemption, personally calling civil rights activists, asking for their forgiveness and admitting he was wrong about segregation. I suspect many politicians who now advocate new coal-fired power plants will also be forced to do some similar soul searching.

Yet without the campaign of civil disobedience in Birmingham, we might still be waiting for white southerners to admit that they were just plain wrong on the issue of civil rights, and that segregation was indeed an immoral institution. The coal industry is today an institution of unparalleled evil, one that threatens our very survival as a species.

Mountaintop removal is an especially destructive form of mining, where the top half of the mountain is literally blasted and chopped off, creating a plateau. The "fill" is pushed into the accompanying hollow by bulldozers, destroying an entire valley and stream. This exposes the coal seam, making tunneling a thing of the past. Mountaintop removal supporters like to point out the benefit of an increase in flat ground in the particularly rugged region.

Local Ed Wiley has seen the bulldozers at work on a spring day. As the dozers moved into a section of black bear dens, Ed saw two young black bears dart out of their homes, only to be crushed and buried alive by debris falling from the bulldozers above. "I wonder how many other bears didn't even make it out of their den," Ed said. You only have to see something like that once to realize that mountaintop removal is one of the most loathsome environmental plagues of our day. All this to mine an archaic fuel source whose very implementation is killing us.

The bears aren't the only creatures on the front line. At Marsh Fork Elementary School, where Ed and Debbie Wiley's granddaughter goes to school, the kids are becoming the casualties in a facility where the water sometimes runs black like the coal sludge stored directly behind the playground. In this case, a gigantic mountaintop removal coal mine surrounds the school area. The building sits 225 feet away from a Massey Energy coal-loading silo that releases high levels of coal dust that saturates the air in the school. A leaking earthen dam holds back 2.8 billion gallons of toxic coal sludge. And Massey wants to build another silo.

Not that Ed and Debbie, or anyone else who sends their child to Marsh Fork Elementary, are going to stand for this. In 2006, Ed, a former coal miner, walked 455 miles to Washington, D.C., to talk to legislators about why they are letting Massey poison his granddaughter.

Despite Gore's call to action, few environmental organizations currently support mass civil disobedience, undoubtedly because of the risks involved. Jail, fines, lawsuits, and the unavoidable charges that they are unreasonable, an accusation that obviously strikes more fear into their hearts than do rising sea levels and mass extinction, have paralyzed environmentalists. There is no better example to support the argument that environmental organizations have become too comfortable and professional, that they're afraid of risks and are hesitant to make any great sacrifice. For us to win this, we will have to change, and change quickly.

Fortunately, some organizations are not afraid. And we should not be too surprised that Earth First! is once again leading the way. On June 30, 2008, thirteen members of Blue Ridge Earth First! became the first group to answer Gore's call. They were arrested for blockading the entrance to Dominion Resources' corporate headquarters in Richmond, Virginia, in protest of the company's plan for a new coal-fired power plant in southwest Virginia.

The Earth First! blockade of Dominion Resources and Tredegar Street, a main Richmond thoroughfare, lasted for more than two hours. The blockade was centered around four college students forming a human chain, their hands encased in containers of hardened cement, the old sleeping dragon trick. Dominion's new plant is projected to release 5.4 million tons of carbon dioxide annually, as well as forty-nine pounds of mercury, and other hazardous chemicals. The plant's demand for coal would also accelerate the rate of mountaintop-removal mining, which has already destroyed 25 percent of the mountains in Wise County, Virginia.

"We've been through the regulatory process, it's time now to take action on our own," declared Hannah Morgan, a nineteen-year-old Earth Firster from Appalachia, a small town in Wise County. On September 15, eleven more protesters were arrested. This time they were joined by the Rainforest Action Network and Asheville Rising Tide, a new international action group committed to fighting climate change.

At the same time as activists were being arrested in Wise County, Rainforest Action Network activists infiltrated Bank of America's thirty-eighth annual investor's conference at the Ritz Hotel in San Francisco. RAN activists hacked into the PowerPoint presentation and projected images of the morning protest, still in progress. Unaware that his PowerPoint had been modified, the presenter waxed on about the bright future of coal as confused murmurs began to emanate from the audience of analysts and investors. Other protests were held in solidarity across the country. The actions received widespread media attention, and the Earth Firsters were joined and supported by many local residents who have come to see the coal companies as predatory and threatening to their future.

With this situation in mind, I decided to make a move to West Virginia, where a battle in Raleigh County was being waged against the opening up of new mountaintop-removal coal mines. I have traveled here many times in the last five years, and have been impressed by the tenacity of the coal industry's local opponents. It's not easy being against coal in a region that has very few good-paying jobs doing anything else.

Local resistance here has been fierce, yet aside from the Earth First!, RAN, and Mountain Justice activists, the only other support from outside has been merely vocal. Many representatives of the big environmental groups, including Robert F. Kennedy Jr., of the Natural Resource Defense Council, have made the trek to Larry Gibson's house on Kayford Mountain. Here mountaintop-removal coal mining surrounds Larry's property, though it's only just begun. Big-name enviros have been to Ed Wiley's house below Coal River Mountain, where Massey wants to mine. So far, none of these leaders have attended any of the demonstrations. In order for the local activists to succeed in their struggle to preserve their mountains, the movement's most visible generals will need to come down to the front line.

The road from my home in Missoula, Montana, to the hills in West Virginia covers more than two thousand miles, but on arrival here, it feels like a different country in a different century. I have most of my meager possessions. The plan is to open up an office in the Coal River Valley to join the campaign. At fifty-four, I'm probably not one of the younger people that Al Gore is talking about, but as a baby boomer, I share my generation's complicity in creating the mess we are in today. Climate change is not a legacy that future generations are likely to forgive us for, nor should they.

The fact is, like most Americans, until very recently I was totally ignorant about coal, its history, and its impact on the world we live in. Coming here is the best way to get an education and, even more important, inspiration. So my first stop is to visit with my friend Larry Gibson. Larry's place on Kayford Mountain serves as a welcome center for the thousands of people who traveled here to see what mountaintop removal looks like up close. Every year Larry throws one of the best parties of the summer both so people can come up and celebrate the beauty of the mountain and to get people as pissed off about mountaintop removal as he is. When I arrived, a band was playing mountain music, and two hundred people were milling about, sampling some of Larry's famous pit barbecue.

I sat down at the table and talked to Larry for a bit. He has been trying to get his neighbors off the coal habit for most of his sixty-some-odd years. Larry's family has owned this property for 250 years, and he has been fighting to save this mountain for a quarter of a century. Larry has had many threats to his life, but he remains unafraid. Both his hat and T-shirt are bright fluorescent green, adorned with anti-strip-mining slogans printed in black boldface type.

"Larry," I said, "doesn't that shirt make you a better target?"

"Well, yes," he responds, "it does." He paused. "But if I won't do it, how can I ask anyone else to?"

Everyone up here on Kayford Mountain feels this way. By coming up to Kayford Mountain, you are not just making a statement, you are also taking a stand on coal, and if you live in the Coal River, you are taking a risk.

Indeed, you cannot be closer to mountaintop removal than

at Larry's, because he is surrounded by the coal mine. This is not the kind of mine you see in the movies. Or even the big open pits you see out West. Here Massey is in the later stages of removing a mountain to get at the coal seams that lie beneath it. Larry's property used to be surrounded by high forested ridges that rose up three hundred feet around his house. Now from the boundary of his place you can gaze down three hundred feet and see the machines still at it, scraping away the bedrock and the dirt into the steep hollows below.

I decide to sit at the edge of his property and watch for a spell. The work continues around the clock, stopping only on Sundays. At about 4:30 P.M. the blasting begins. Hundreds of bore holes are drilled into the bedrock, filled with dynamite, and detonated, causing the ground to tremor and explode, sending a thunderous noise down the valley. Afterwards dust clouds billow high above the truncated mountain. When a new work shift begins, a large dragline methodically removes gravel from the blast area and loads it into a truck bed. The line of trucks is long. They take the material to the valley and dump it, where bulldozers push it over the side of the mountain and into the creek below. Without pause, the trucks return, beeping and growling, to be loaded again, in endless repetition, shaving off one layer of the mountain after another, until the thin seam of coal is exposed. The dragline will then load this coal into the trucks, and the material will be taken to a processing plant, washed in chemical detergents, and loaded on trains that will take it to virtually every corner of the Earth.

I sat there and watched until after midnight. What I was witnessing has to be among the greatest crimes against nature ever committed. A mountain that has been here for millions of years, indeed one of the oldest mountains on Earth, was disappearing before my eyes. Also disappearing was one of the oldest and most biologically diverse forests ever to exist and, along with it, a people and a way of life, people whose families fought in the American Revolution. People who fought for workers' rights against the coal companies, sparking a labor movement here that changed working conditions not only in the coal mines, but also in factories, mills, and smelters across the country.

Already, as much as a fourth of the mountains in this part of West Virginia have been destroyed by mountaintop removal. The large machines now in use have displaced the coal miner. One dragline, operated by a small crew, can do the work of six hundred underground coal miners. The displaced miners often have no other choice but to head out of state to find jobs in the factories in the big industrial cities.

The coal and the people are leaving the county, but much is left behind. High dams impound the overburden formerly known as a valley. The toxic sludge left over from processing sits in large holding ponds above the pristine rivers of Appalachia. If one of these dams breaks, the sludge will kill every fish from the mountains to the ocean. It is hard to square this bleak reality with the claims of the coal companies that they are following the law. They aren't, but in my opinion, the laws are either not being enforced or are ineffective.

There have been a slew of environmental laws passed in order to prevent such a catastrophe, but just like the mine-safety laws designed to protect the workers, they are rarely obeyed, and paying fines is viewed as cheaper than complying. When confronted with a coal company's malfeasance, sympathetic judges and politicians simply look the other way. That is the way it has always been in West Virginia.

Coal is big money here in Appalachia. Yet West Virginia is among the poorest regions in America. The money goes to mine owners and other investors, many of whom have never seen a coal mine, and little thought is given to the local economy, or to the future. The thinking is that coal will always be big here, and there is no reason to change.

Changes are on the horizon. They will have a profound effect on West Virginia. The reduction of carbon dioxide emissions to address climate change will put climate change and coal mining on a collision course. If we continue to burn coal at the rate we do today, what remains of one of the Appalachians will be destroyed, as well as the air we breathe. There are no easy answers to climate change, but if there is an answer, it must be found here in places like West Virginia, where a standing forest can store over forty tons of carbon per acre per year. It is insanity to think that these mountains have less value than the seam of coal that underlies them.

The two most critical steps we need to take to reduce these emissions are to stop burning coal and to preserve the remaining forests. There is an urgent need to reduce carbon dioxide emissions by 90 percent or more in the coming decades, which will be no small task, and every country on Earth is going to have to get involved if we wish to make any progress toward this goal. If the United States is not willing to sacrifice in order to meet this goal, there is scant reason to believe that China, India, or Russia will either, and that is precisely why European countries are now trying to reduce their own emissions.

In spite of all the concern over what these rising CO_2 levels have in store for humanity, levels are continuing to increase. The world's emissions rose 3 percent in the year from 2006 to 2007, setting a course that could push beyond the worst-case scenario projected by a Nobel Prize–winning group of international scientists. This includes a hundred-foot sea level rise by the end of the century, or possibly sooner—and sea levels are rising now at a rate of three centimeters a year, and that rate is increasing. Already, beaches and coastal wetlands are disappearing, with a drastic effect on fish and wildlife. It is well past time for serious action.

The good news is that even here in West Virginia, attitudes toward climate change are changing, and most residents here now favor alternatives like wind and solar power over mining any more coal. Still, a good 38 percent of residents continue to favor burning coal. Environmentalists have their work cut out for them in their efforts to stop the opening of new coal mines here in Raleigh County, where a big battle now looms over the fate of Coal River Mountain. Massey Energy, which has purchased the mineral rights, is planning to remove the entire mountain, which is visible from the back porch of Ed Wiley's house. The Coal River, which runs past his house, finds its headwaters on the mountain slated for removal. Removing the mountain will mean the destruction of Ed's drinking water, and the Coal River will be little more than a sewer funneling mining waste downhill, poisoning all in its path.

Local residents, led by the Ohio Valley Environmental Coalition in Huntington, are proposing a wind farm for the ridge on Coal Mountain where Massey wants to mine. This project will not only produce electricity in perpetuity, but will also capture a significant amount of carbon in the biomass. It will create good jobs, leave the mountain intact, the fish in the streams, and the black bears in their dens.

The wind proposal is generating some real excitement in the Coal River Valley, and the stage is set for a showdown. On one side of the line is a clean-energy future, and a solution to climate change. On the other side, more wanton destruction of our natural environment for the dirtiest energy imaginable. It's time to walk the line. And it's time to get off your couch and help people like Ed Wiley and Larry Gibson salvage what's left of the Appalachians.

Today, the environmental movement has entered a new phase. It's gone global, and its ranks now include world leaders, celebrities, and multinational corporations. Yet, citizen action is needed more than ever.

Al Gore is on board. In an August 16, 2007, *New York Times* column, Gore was quoted telling Nicholas Kristof, "We are now treating the Earth's atmosphere as an open sewer. I can't understand why there aren't rings of young people blocking bulldozers, and preventing them from constructing coal-fired power plants."

In this case, I agree with Al Gore. I just wish he would put his money where his mouth is. I ask you to join me in the effort to take to task the big corporate polluters and robbers. It's not too late. Your action can change the course of the world.